Listen Up!

Listen Up!
PODCASTING *for* Schools *and* Libraries

Linda W. Braun

Information Today, Inc.
Medford, New Jersey

First printing, 2007

Listen Up! Podcasting for Schools and Libraries

Library of Congress Cataloging-in-Publication Data

Braun, Linda W.
Listen up! : podcasting for schools and libraries / Linda W. Braun.
p. cm.
Includes bibliographical references and index.
ISBN-13: 978-1-57387-304-8
1. Internet in education. 2. Internet in libraries. 3. Podcasting. I. Title
LB1044.87.B722 2007
371.33'4678--dc22

2007023650

President and CEO: Thomas H. Hogan, Sr.
Editor-in-Chief and Publisher: John B. Bryans
Managing Editor: Amy M. Reeve
Project Editor: Rachel Singer Gordon
VP Graphics and Production: M. Heide Dengler
Book Designer: Kara Mia Jalkowski
Cover Designer: Shelley Szajner
Copyeditor: Pat Hadley-Miller
Proofreader: Barbara Brynko
Indexer: Beth Palmer

Dedication

One more time for Robert, all by himself,
for helping me get this done

Contents

APPENDIX B

APPENDIX C

About the Web Site www.leonline.com/listen_up

The *Listen Up! Podcasting for Schools and Libraries* Web site gives easy access to the podcasts and podcast resources mentioned in this book. The site is a resource for learning about creating podcasts and provides links to everything a podcaster needs in order to get a podcast production up and running. The site also allows readers to download a list of podcast subscriptions for import into their own podcast listening software—a quick way to get started listening to and analyzing podcasts.

Disclaimer

Neither the publisher nor the author makes any claim as to the results that may be obtained through the use of this Web site or of any of the Internet resources it references or links to. Neither publisher nor author will be held liable for any results, or lack thereof, obtained by the use of this page or any of its links; for any third-party changes; or for any hardware, software, or other problems that may occur as the result of using it. This Web site is subject to change or discontinuation without notice at the discretion of the publisher and author.

Foreword

I am not a teacher, but I play one on TV. Neither am I a librarian, but information is my stock in trade. I am a Leo, but not a LEO. For the past 30 years I've been a radio broadcaster, for the past 15 years I've been a television host, but I've been a podcaster for just three years. Of course, podcasting itself isn't much older, but it stands on the shoulders of its older siblings: radio and TV. Of the three, it's by far my favorite medium.

If, like me, you love information and have a calling to help others learn, then you should consider podcasting as one of the truly useful tools in your kit. In this book you will learn about the most exciting new medium since Gutenberg began pressing ink into paper. The term "podcast" is a combination of "iPod"—the ubiquitous audio gadget most commonly used to play podcasts—and "broadcast"—its big brother medium. I've also heard it said that the POD in podcasting should stand for "portable on-demand"—and that, in a nutshell, is what people like so much about podcasts.

Podcasts are shows you can bring with you wherever you go, and listen to or watch whenever you want. They're the ultimate form of media for the fast food generation, but they can be much more mentally nutritious. Podcasts are about giving people what they want: entertainment and information in a convenient form.

Better still, with the help of this book, you'll find that podcasts are easy to make. Once you grasp the idea, you'll find yourself cranking them out faster than the Colonel can whip out a bucket of chicken. Using the techniques outlined here, I have produced more than 1,000 podcast episodes in the past three years; these days, I average more than 10 a week. More than 4 million people listen to my shows each month, and it costs me next to nothing to produce them. For a long time, I created podcasts with just the equipment I found lying around the office. I only wish I had had this book when I was starting out. I've had to learn all this stuff the hard way: by trial and error—mostly error!

Now that I'm a bigshot podcaster (an oxymoron if there ever was one), people often ask me for the secret to podcasting success. This depends on how you define success, of course, but if your goal is to communicate, to reach people, to excite, to empower, to entertain, or to inform, then the secret is simple: Podcast your passion. Make your podcast about the things you care about the most. If you bring your passion to your show, everything else will follow. Share your knowledge and your enthusiasm, and people will embrace you.

In this book, Linda Braun has compiled everything else you need to know in order to begin your media career. You'll find technical details, useful tips, information on what to buy, and, perhaps more importantly, what you don't need to spend money on. This is the most comprehensive book yet on the medium of podcasting, and it's designed just for you. So get going. I, and the world, await your show. I just know it's going to be great.

Leo Laporte
Founder and producer of the TWiT Netcast Network (twit.tv)
Nationally syndicated radio talk show host,
The Tech Guy on Premiere Radio Networks
Host, the Lab with Leo on G4TechTV Canada
and the How-To Network in Australia

Introduction

When I talk to friends, family, students, and colleagues about podcasting, I regularly tell them that I love podcasting and that podcasting changed my life. Neither statement is an exaggeration.

- I love podcasting because it provides opportunities to hear what people—who I might otherwise never get a chance to hear—have to say.
- I love podcasting because it opens up a world of content that goes beyond what I have access to elsewhere.
- Podcasting changed my life because I have control over what I listen to or watch and when I listen to or watch it.
- Podcasting changed my life because I can listen or watch almost anywhere: on my way to an appointment, on the subway, in a car, or while doing chores around the house.
- Podcasting changed my life because I learn better by listening than by reading. I tend to remember nonfiction content that I hear, when I wouldn't necessarily remember it if I read it.
- Podcasting changed my life because, when I don't feel like reading after spending hours sitting in front of a computer every day, I can still enjoy content via a podcast.

Use of the Term "Podcasting"

Throughout this book, I use podcast as a generic term to describe casts containing either audio or video content.

Since I started listening to and watching podcasts, I've changed the way I access content, both for learning and entertainment. I've changed the way I keep abreast of current trends, news, and even historic events. I do less leisure reading than I used to; instead, I often spend my leisure time listening to and watching podcast productions by people who aren't professionals in the mainstream media world. They aren't going to ever make it big in Hollywood, but they have interesting and entertaining things to say.

The Rest of the World

In a study published in November 2006, the Pew Internet and American Life Project[1] found a large increase in the percentage of people who had downloaded a podcast between April and November 2006. In April, 7 percent of those interviewed by Pew had downloaded a podcast. By November, 12 percent had downloaded a podcast.

At the same time that the number of people downloading podcasts is increasing, so too is the number of podcasts that are available for listening or viewing. The Pew report notes that, as of late 2006, the Podcast Alley directory (www.podcastalley.com) listed 26,000 podcasts. For those podcasts, it lists more than 1 million episodes. According to Pew, in November 2004, there were just 1,000 podcasts.

When people first started talking about podcasting, there was a lot of discussion about whether this way of delivering content was just a fad. The fact that the audience continues to grow, the technology is more mainstream, and more and more podcasts debut on a regular basis are signs that this is not a fad. Given the growing importance of the medium, librarians and educators need to pay attention, learn what podcasting is, and find ways to integrate it into the work that they do.

What About Schools and Libraries?

Podcasting is a tool that can be used both to deliver information and to build a sense of community. For example, a librarian might want to support the needs of local 20-somethings more successfully. One way to do so would be with a podcast geared just to that age group. In this podcast, the librarian might talk about the services available for 20-somethings. She might visit community agencies and businesses that cater to that population, using the podcast to introduce these institutions to the audience. This fits into libraries' role: providing helpful information targeted to a specific group.

Podcasting is also a tool that can be used to put a human face on a person or institution. For example, imagine that a school principal hosts a weekly podcast in which she talks about the books she is reading, her philosophy on education, the community events she is involved in, and the interesting news she's heard related to teaching and learning over the past week. Listeners would get to see the principal in a role other than that of school rule maker and disciplinarian. Listeners would hear the principal as an individual who has particular interests and philosophies. They would get to know her as someone who participates in community activities outside of school. They would view her as someone who is willing to let others in on what she thinks and knows.

How *Listen Up! Podcasting for Schools and Libraries* Can Help

Listen Up! Podcasting for Schools and Libraries is a good way for those in both types of institutions to begin learning about what podcasting is and how to go out and create podcasts. It demystifies some of the technology behind podcasting and explains and demonstrates that anyone can get a podcast up and running, without much expense, and with just a small amount of technical expertise.

A starter guide, *Listen Up!* gives readers ideas on how to find podcasts, about what's available, and on what goes into creating a podcast. This is not a technical manual on podcasting, but it lists the steps you need to get started and provides information on where to get the technical help and support you might need.

Listen Up! also includes ideas throughout on topics that library and school podcasters might try out for themselves. It includes interviews with librarians who are already podcasting. It's focused on the real world of podcasting and what a school staff member or librarian could actually accomplish.

What's Inside

Each chapter covers a different aspect of podcasting, from what podcasting is (and what it isn't) to what a library or school needs to do in order to get people listening to their podcast productions.

Chapter 1 defines podcasting. This overview chapter includes information on how to find and listen to podcasts, plus information on the history of podcasts. If you are already familiar with podcasting, you still might read this chapter to be reminded of some things your co-workers may have questions about. If you are a complete novice to podcasting, Chapter 1 gives you the information you need to understand what the technology is all about and helps you learn how to explain it to others.

Chapter 2 focuses on the reasons libraries and schools should get into podcasting and on ways to plan for podcasting within an institution. It provides 10 reasons why podcasting makes sense for libraries and other educational institutions and outlines the issues that need to be considered before producing your first podcast.

Chapter 3 lists a number of podcasts that are worth listening to or watching in order to get ideas about what works and what doesn't work. These podcasts represent a small set of examples within a small set of topics—professional development, education, technology, humor, and entertainment. (As mentioned previously, listeners have tens of thousands of podcasts to choose from.)

Chapter 4 is all about what it takes to make a good podcast, focusing on the content and organization of the production. In this chapter, you'll read about podcast formats, learn how to locate music for use in a podcast, and find out about the importance of a podcast companion Web site.

Chapter 5 looks at the technology behind podcasting. This chapter discusses devices such as microphones and video cameras, including tips on factors to consider when purchasing these pieces of hardware. Chapter 5 also includes instructions on recording and editing podcast content, what to think about when finding a place for your podcast to live, and how to let listeners and viewers know whenever a new podcast episode is available.

Chapter 6 focuses on how to get people to actually listen to or view your podcast. It covers techniques to use in order to attract and keep listeners, and looks at using traditional and new technologies to get the word out about your production.

Appendix A contains a podcast planning checklist that helps you think through the how and why of the podcast you want to produce. Appendix B provides a list of tools and links to them. You might use these to produce and distribute a podcast. Appendix C provides an example of XML in a podcast feed, highlighting the aspects of the feed that tell subscribers what's available in the newest podcast available for download.

Change Happens

In the early days of podcasting, audio was it. Now, those who prefer audio-visual communication have the choice of video podcasts. Over time, podcasting will continue to grow and change in the same way that all technology does. Already, as I note in Chapter 1, some software programs are providing automatic file-saving options for delivering files to an iPod or other portable media devices; podcasts are also being used in popular virtual worlds such as Second Life.

It's impossible to look into a crystal ball to see what podcasting will look like in five years. However, podcasting itself is a huge change in the ways content is delivered to users so they can access it whenever needed or wanted. That change is what schools and libraries need to focus on. No matter what podcasting may look like in the future, we need to start exploring podcasts and the technology behind them today.

Endnote

1. Pew Internet and American Life Project, "Pew Internet Project Data Memo: Podcast Downloading," www.pewinternet.org/pdfs/PIP_Podcasting.pdf (2006).

CHAPTER 1

This Thing We Call Podcasting

About two years ago, as the popular press started to cover podcasting, my husband said to me: "I don't get it. I've been able to download audio files on the Web for years. What makes podcasting different?" My response was: "You're right about Web-based audio. The thing is that podcasting is about more than the ability to access and download audio on the Web. What makes podcasting different is that listeners can subscribe to the audio and have it delivered to their computers automatically." As Wikipedia notes: "What makes podcasting distinct from other digital audio and video delivery is the use of syndication feed enclosures."[1]

I also told my husband that one of the other great things about podcasting was the homegrown nature of content distributed via the Web. Ordinary people could easily record audio, get it posted on a Web site, and make it available on a subscription basis. In the early days of podcasting, before much of the mainstream media made their content available via podcasts, amateur media producers began creating audio podcasts on topics of importance to them. We saw podcasts just for mothers by mothers, podcasts just for fathers by fathers, podcasts from fans of particular TV shows, and so on. We can still access these types of podcasts, but, along with all this homegrown content, now we can also choose from lots of professionally produced content created by traditional media such as movie studios, television stations, and radio networks. Even though podcasting has grown and changed over the past couple of years, it's important to remember that the early days of podcasting were very much about the ability for anyone with something to say to create their own radio show. An understanding of the homegrown roots of the medium helps librarians and educators understand that they can produce and distribute podcasts along with NPR, the *New York Times*, and C|NET.

Podcast FAQ

What is a podcast?
Podcasts are regularly produced audio and video files that are available for subscription and that can automatically be downloaded to a computer and/or portable audio and video device.

Do I need to have an iPod to listen to podcasts?
No, you can listen to podcasts on a computer or almost any MP3 device.

Does a subscription cost anything?
Usually not.

Where do I find out about podcasts?
You can search for podcasts in many places, including the iTunes Music Store (www.apple.com/itunes/store/podcasts.html), Odeo (www.odeo.com), and Yahoo! Podcasts (podcasts. yahoo.com).

What do I need to subscribe to a podcast?
A piece of software or online tool called a podcatcher. These include software such as iTunes and Web-based tools such as Odeo.

What do I need to transfer a podcast to a portable media device?
If you have an iPod, you can use iTunes. For other devices, you can use podcatchers such as Juice (juicereceiver.sourceforge.net/index.php) and jPodder (www.jpodder.com).

How can I make sure others find the podcast that I produce?
Get it listed in the various podcatching databases. Be sure to submit it to iTunes, Odeo, and Yahoo! Podcasts.

Now, two years after I had that discussion with my husband, librarians regularly tell me they are producing podcasts. This is encouraging.

However, what these librarians are actually doing in most cases is creating audio files, uploading them to the Web, and making them available to their patrons from their library's Web pages. These files aren't podcasts in the pure sense of the word. They often aren't available for subscription, nor are they pushed to a subscriber's computer and automatically downloaded on a regular basis. Why are librarians simply creating the audio and not taking the next step? This is perhaps because they don't know how to take the next step. It's become fairly easy to create the audio files, but making these files subscription-based is not quite as simple.

Before getting into creating subscription-based audio files, though, we need to back up a bit. A brief discussion of the history and technology behind podcasting will provide some helpful context.

Podcasting's Roots

I first read about podcasting in early 2005. At the time, I didn't realize the technology was already a few years old. The "History of Podcasting" Wikipedia article, quoted previously, explains that the concept of podcasting first appeared in the fall of 2000. The idea was that audio files could be delivered to computers via an RSS feed that included an enclosure. (Read on to find out what these terms and phrases actually mean.)

What's an RSS Feed?

RSS stands for "Really Simple Syndication" or "Rich Site Survey." An RSS feed makes it possible to subscribe to Web content in order to find out whenever something new has been added to a given site. The news that there is new material on a blog or Web site is automatically fed (pushed) to an individual's computer. For example, I like to read Ypulse (www.ypulse.com), which provides daily news and commentary about Generation Y. Instead of having to regularly check the site to see if something new is posted, I subscribe to its RSS feed. Whenever there's new information on the site, my feed reader lets me know.

What's a Feed Reader?

In order to get updates when new information is posted on a blog or Web site, I have to use either a piece of software on my computer or a Web-based tool that will let me know the new content exists. That software or Web-based tool is called a feed reader. When one of my feeds contains new content, the feed reader lets me know by showing new headlines within the reader window on my computer screen, as shown in Figure 1.1.

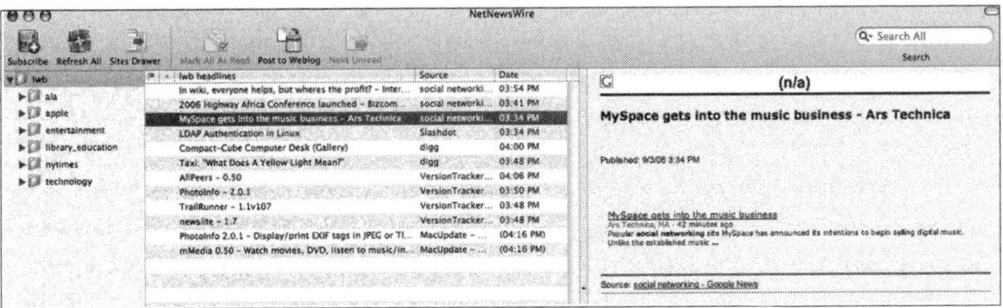

Figure 1.1 Sample headlines list from a feed reader

When I set up my feed reader to check up on the sites that interest me, I am subscribing to the feeds for those sites. Not all Web sites or blogs have feeds, but you can tell which ones do by looking for one of the logos that usually accompany an RSS feed subscription link. Figure 1.2 shows examples of common RSS feed logos.

Figure 1.2 Sample RSS feed logos

What's an Enclosure?

When I receive an RSS feed—in other words, when I am alerted by my feed reader that there is new content on the Ypulse Web site (or another one of my subscriptions)—I'm not actually downloading anything from Ypulse to my computer. Instead, my feed reader just shows me an excerpt of the new Ypulse content on my computer screen, with a link I can click on to view the full content.

With a podcast, instead of Web or blog content, the feed reader (which, for podcasts, is called a "podcatcher") downloads an "enclosure"—read on to learn about enclosures.

How to Subscribe to an RSS Feed

To receive updates whenever new information is posted to a favorite Web site or blog that supports RSS, you need to subscribe to the site's feed. The exact way you subscribe to feeds depends on the tool you use to read them; however, the basic steps and concept remain the same from tool to tool:

1. Click on the subscribe, RSS, XML, or syndication link on the site to which you want to subscribe. (See Figure 1.2 for examples of RSS feed logos.)
2. In most cases, this leads you to a new page that shows the XML content for the feed. Ignore this, and look at the URL in the address bar of your Web browser—that's all you need to subscribe to the feed. Copy the URL by highlighting it and clicking Edit ... Copy.
3. Open up your feed reader and select the option for adding a new feed. (This is often labeled "Add Feed" or "Add New Subscription." You might also see a button with a + on it.)
4. Paste in the URL of the feed by clicking Edit ... Paste.

You will then be subscribed to the feed in your feed reader.

Podcatchers, Podcatching, and Enclosures

The key technological innovation that first made podcasting possible was the capability to enclose a file, called an enclosure, in an RSS feed. RSS feeds had been available for a while, but in the early 2000s, the technology that allowed enclosures was pretty new. By the way, these enclosures aren't just for audio. Once it was possible to include files as a part of an RSS feed, it was also possible to include video content. Today it is just as easy (and there is no difference in the process) to subscribe to a videocast (also known as vidcast, video blog, or vodcast) as to an audio-only podcast.

Podcasting didn't really start gaining notice and interest from a larger audience—such as the mainstream media, educators, and musicians—until fall 2004 and early 2005. In summer 2005, Apple updated the iTunes music store with software to support podcasts. That was a big step toward bringing podcasting into the mainstream, because iTunes is such an easy-to-use podcatcher. iTunes was not the first podcatcher, and it's definitely not the only one. But, because of Apple's dominance in the MP3 marketplace and the world of downloadable audio content, iTunes is often the only podcatcher listeners know about—and therefore use.

Not only is iTunes a podcatcher, but it is also a podcast directory. Users can search for podcasts and find what they want to catch using the same software, making iTunes an all-in-one tool for podcasting users. Sometimes people are confused by the use of iTunes as a podcast directory, thinking this means Apple has some control over the podcast content. In most cases, though, that's not true. Podcasts are included in the iTunes music store (or in any other podcast directory) because podcasters have submitted their content to that directory. Podcasters can submit a podcast to a directory manually (filling out a form within the software or Web site) and/or add code to a podcast's feed in order to get it listed in specific podcast directories. Read more about podcast directories later in this chapter.

Podcast Subscriptions

A podcast, to truly be a podcast, needs to be produced and published on a somewhat regular schedule, be available for download, be subscription-based, and support an RSS feed with enclosures. Earlier, I mentioned that many libraries probably don't make their audio files subscription-based because they get stuck on creating the RSS feed (which will be discussed in more detail in later chapters). In a nutshell, an RSS feed requires an XML file that informs the feed reader about the content that is being fed. This information includes the podcast's title, keywords or tags, whether or not enclosures are included, podcatcher-specific information, and so on. See Appendix C for more information on what an XML file for a podcast looks like.

Since not everyone has the ability to manually create an XML file and maintain an RSS feed, a number of Web sites will host a podcast, create a feed for you, and distribute the feed to subscribers. One of these is PodServe (www.pod-serve.com), a free service from Biggu. All podcast creators need to do is register, set up a section for their podcast on the PodServe site, and upload new podcasts as they are created; PodServe does the rest. (See Chapter 5 for more information on creating a podcast and setting up a podcast distribution mechanism.)

Just as icons on Web pages alert viewers to the availability of RSS feeds, there are also icons that act as an alert to podcast availability. See Figure 1.3 for examples of podcast subscription logos.

Figure 1.3 Sample podcast subscription logos

Finding, Listening, and Being Found

As mentioned previously, users have their choice among many tools for finding podcasts. First, listeners can browse and search the podcast section of the iTunes Music Store. (Remember, even though it's called a store, most of the podcasts found in the iTunes Music Store—and most podcasts in general—are free.) Odeo is another Web site for finding, subscribing, and listening to podcasts, and Yahoo! Podcasts is both a directory of podcasts and a place where people can listen to podcasts.

In the same way that Web site owners want their sites to rise to the top in search engine result lists, podcast creators want their podcasts to show up in directories such as the iTunes music store, Odeo, and Yahoo! Podcasts, as well as in the other places listeners use to find casts and subscribe to them. As with sites that search the Web, there are different ways to make sure a podcast is included and indexed well in these directories. Podcast producers can submit their podcasts to iTunes, Odeo, and others to make sure the cast is listed. (Chapter 6 focuses on how to market your podcast and includes more information on getting listed in podcast directories.)

When thinking about where people find podcasts, it's important to also think about how they listen to them. The three podcatchers mentioned previously are also tools for listening to podcasts on a computer. However, one reason for podcasts' popularity is that they are easily transferable to a portable audio device, whether an iPod or any other variety of MP3 player. (Note that not all podcatchers will work with all MP3 players, however.) The portability of podcasts is the key to their success. People can plug in their player, download the latest podcasts, stick the player in a pocket, and hit the road. They can listen at work, on their daily walk or jog, or while doing household chores.

Ongoing Developments

Nothing is static: Even as this book goes to press, new technologies and trends are expanding the way podcasts are used in schools and libraries. For example:

- As a part of the podcast creation process, most producers also set up a Web site, blog, or wiki that supports and supplements the content of the production. The distribution of an audio or video file is just the start of the dissemination of information or the entertainment experience. More and more people are finding ways to enhance listening and viewing, including features like interactive Web-based components, the ability to provide audio feedback, polls related to content in the current episode, and the ability to create a transcript of the episode via a wiki or other collaborative content development tool. (See Chapter 4 for more information on podcast companion Web sites.)
- As mentioned previously, video podcasts are not a distant pipe dream; they are here and now. The introduction of the iPod with video made it easier for viewers to take video podcasts on the road, and more and more companies are now coming out with their own versions of video-capable portable players.
- Enhanced podcasts are an invention of Apple, but more and more devices and creators will likely be able to integrate them. Enhanced podcasts allow viewers to view specific content on the screen based on what they hear at a particular moment in a podcast. For example, while listening to a podcast of a library tour, the listener might see different rooms of the library based on what the narrator of the podcast is saying at any particular moment. Enhanced podcasts also allow listeners to move forward from chapter to chapter within a podcast, as opposed to simply fast-forwarding without really knowing precisely where the fast-forward will end up.
- Non-podcast-specific software includes portable device extensions or plug-ins. For example, Kid Pix Studio (drawing software often used in elementary school classrooms) includes a conversion option, allowing Kid Pix Studio files

to be transferred easily to an iPod or another portable media device with video and image capabilities. This means that any Kid Pix movie, slide show, or drawing a student creates can be viewed on a portable device by a parent.

- Educational institutions are creating tutorials that are viewable on video and image capable portable devices. For example, a teacher or librarian might create a tutorial on how to use a particular Web site or electronic resource. That tutorial can be exported in a format compatible with video devices, so that students can access it when sitting in a café, walking through the library stacks, or hanging out in a park. The learning goes with the student from classroom to library to park to café to home. (See Chapter 5 for more on creating how-to vidcasts.)
- Podcasts are tied into specific events. For example, movie studios now create podcasts that coincide with the production of a particular film, making them available on a regular basis during filming.
- Podcasts are moving into virtual environments. Second Life (www.secondlife.com) is a popular virtual space where people of all ages go to take classes, listen to lectures, go to parties, hang out with others, go to the library, visit Amazon, and so on. It is possible to podcast from Second Life, and this is likely to become more and more popular over time.
- People are listening to podcasts over the phone. No longer do podcast listeners have to be tied to portable media devices or computers; instead, they can use their phones to listen. One service that provides this capability is Podlinez (www.podlinez.com). The important point here is that, as more and more opportunities for podcast listening appear, more and more people will spend time listening—and will know what podcasts are all about.
- Searching through audio is becoming mainstream. Podzinger (www.podzinger.com) is one of the tools that lets users search through audio content. That means that not only can listeners and potential listeners search for

ideas presented in audio content, but they can also actually search for words spoken within a podcast.

Programmers, producers, listeners, and viewers continue to come up with exciting ways to expand and extend podcasting technology and push the technology envelope. Don't forget that the early days of podcasting were really about the common man being able to create audio content and get it out for the world to hear. This is still true, and what podcasts also allow anyone to do is to determine his or her own audio programming. Having access to podcasts is like having a radio station filled just with content of interest to a particular listener—who doesn't even have to hear a show at the time it airs on the radio, but can listen in his or her own time. This is personal listening, and it's listening that is really focused on people's particular interests and needs. Podcasting makes it possible for people to hear the shows what they want to hear, when they want to hear them. The next few chapters of this book will help you learn about podcasting your own content, so you can support the desires of listeners and viewers to create a personal, portable media world.

Endnote

1. Wikipedia, "History of Podcasting," en.wikipedia.org/wiki/History_of_podcasting (accessed December 13, 2006).

Before You Get Started

Schools and libraries that implement podcasting have a variety of reasons for doing so. It's important to start by determining why and how podcasting makes sense for you. Hennepin County (MN) Library Web services librarian Meg Canada says: "It was a new way to incorporate teen produced content into the Web site,"[1] while Dowling College (NY) digital resources librarian Chris Kretz implemented podcasting "as a way to promote the library and its activities in a new and exciting way."[2]

Why Podcasting Makes Sense for Schools and Libraries

When thinking about integrating any new technology into schools and libraries, it's important to be able to articulate to administrators, peers, colleagues, and the community at large why the new technology makes sense within the context of the institution's programs and services. To get you started, here are 10 reasons why podcasting is an appropriate option for libraries and schools to consider:

1. Get information about programs and services out to the community. Librarians constantly tell me that customers—no matter their age—are overscheduled. Users often don't have time to get to the library to find out what's going on. They don't tend to visit the library's Web site for anything more than finding a book in the online catalog. If the customers aren't coming to the library because they just don't have the time, the library should go to where their customers are. They may be in their cars, walking down the street, waiting in a line, or doing household chores. A library can make it possible for users to find out about services, resources, and programs via an audio (or video) file that can be transferred to a portable media device.

Teachers similarly mention that parents don't always have a good idea about what's really going on in their child's classroom. A weekly update on current projects and assignments, along with information on decisions about everything from desk setup to recess plans, can help improve communication between parents and teachers. Delivering that information in an easily accessible format makes sense for families juggling work, school, and play.

2. Demonstrate the positive aspects and uses of current technologies. All too often, librarians and educators hear about the harmful impact of new technologies on learning, teaching, and literacy. Library and classroom podcasts are a great way to show that it is possible to use new technologies to improve the lives of students. Librarians might create weekly book review podcasts that highlight either curriculum-related or pleasure-reading choices, or teachers might have students deliver reports in podcast format. Each of these examples demonstrates a way in which technology can be used to enhance and extend learning.

3. Use the technology to teach the technology. By producing subscription-based and regularly updated podcasts, educators give adults, teens, and children opportunities to use RSS feeds, podcatchers, and MP3 devices. In order to listen to the podcast, at a minimum, users have to know how to download an audio file. More advanced users will need to learn how to subscribe to an RSS feed and transfer an audio file to an MP3 device.

   When producing podcasts, you can make a point of getting members of the community—adults and/or children—involved in the production. They might help create and edit the audio file. Or, they might work on developing a Web site that provides information on the podcast, with regular alerts as new episodes are released.

4. Bring outside perspectives to the community. Schools and libraries frequently host speakers, but it can be difficult for members of the community to attend at the scheduled time. Library staff members, faculty members, or administrators sometimes also have the opportunity to talk with someone whose viewpoints might be interesting

to the community (such as an author or person of local interest). Podcasts of both formal presentations and informal conversations are great ways to give members of the library or school audience a chance to encounter people and ideas they might not otherwise come into contact with.

5. Show the library or school as a venue for learning, recreation, and entertainment. All too often, the people who support educational institutions within a specific community, such as taxpayers, students, or faculty, do so within a very limited frame of reference. For example, most adults state that it's important for a community (whether that community be a town or educational institution) to have a library, but they can't always articulate why—except in general, warm, and fuzzy terms. By integrating podcasts into their programs and services, libraries and schools have the chance to educate community members, in an appealing format, about the benefits of their institution.

6. Let listeners know about cool, interesting, or new things going on and available in the broader world. Wouldn't it be great if the library or school podcast was one of the resources people thought of first when trying to keep up in the realm of learning, reading, and information? Podcasts work really well as tools for keeping on top of what's going on. For example, I know that the Buzz Out Loud (alpha.cnet.com) podcast is one of my best sources for weekly technology-related news. I know that if I don't have time to read the newspaper or technology blogs for a couple of days during any given week, I can still stay up-to-date because of Buzz Out Loud. Shouldn't people in the community in which you work feel the same way about the content of your podcasts? If you do a "This week in reading" or "This week in learning" podcast, you become the main source for that information for the people who listen to your podcast.

7. Give the community a chance to get to know teachers, faculty, librarians, and administrators as individuals. Often the people who work in a school or library don't seem "real" to the members of the community they serve. Podcasts can be a way to change that. Weekly podcasts might include a librarian talking about what she's currently reading, as a

way to present her personality to the community. Or, a school's podcast might include interviews with faculty and staff who can talk about interests, hobbies, or what they're reading.

8. Help people make connections. When I listen to the same podcast as my peers, I am able to have a "water-cooler" experience. I know several people who also listen to Diggnation (revision3.com/diggnation). After we listen to (or view) the latest episode, we can have a conversation about the topics covered.

   Perhaps after creating podcasts for your library or school you can host programs at your institution where listeners get together to talk about ideas, books, and the other topics covered. Or maybe, after a podcast is distributed, the Web site you create can provide listeners with an opportunity to comment on content included in the latest digital download. In other words, don't assume that once a podcast is distributed that this will be the end of the experience for the producers or the listeners.

9. Update staff on what's happening in the institution. Podcasts don't have to be just for the outside community; they can also be used as internal tools for communication. Podcast technology is a great way to give staff information about happenings in the organization, initiate discussion on new policies and projects, and introduce new staff members to the rest of the organization. By using podcasts as internal communication tools, you give staff members the chance to use new technology and to learn about what's going on at a time convenient to them.

10. Provide multiple formats for learning. When I was growing up, classroom lectures, printed text, filmstrips, and still images were my primary options for learning about a topic. Now, students of all ages have the opportunity to learn through a number of different formats. By producing podcasts, along with traditional forms of content dissemination, you give current learners the chance to understand ideas in the format (or multiple formats) that makes the most sense to them.

The following chapters include a variety of podcast examples and provide information on how to create a podcast from scratch. Before getting into that, however, not only is it important to focus on the why of podcasts, but also on what you need to think about before producing and launching your first cast.

Planning for Podcasting

Before you jump gung-ho into producing podcasts for your community, it's a good idea to sit down with colleagues to talk about the development, production, and publication of your potential podcast. Use the podcast planning worksheet in Appendix A to help jumpstart your discussions, and the sidebar on this page will help stimulate your ideas on the various types of podcasts schools and libraries might think about implementing.

Ten Types of Library and School Podcasts

1. *Public event* – Recordings of library- and school-sponsored events, such as speakers and performances, are a good way to allow those who can't attend these events to participate. Remember, though, if you are going to record public events sponsored by your library or school, it's important to get permission from the presenters to publish the recording as a podcast.
2. *Book discussion groups* – Schools and libraries frequently host book discussion groups for a wide variety of age groups. Why not record these discussions and make them available as podcasts? This gives people who attended the opportunity to reconsider the discussion and gives those who couldn't attend the opportunity to hear what people have to say about a particular book.
3. *Interviews* – Every community has people with great stories to tell. Consider producing those stories as podcast interviews. Library staff, teachers, students, or teens could produce the podcasts, making it

possible for people in the community to learn about each other and their stories.

4. *What's happening this week* – Teachers, librarians, and faculty can produce podcasts about what's going on in the classroom or library over the next week. This is a good way to keep parents and community members up-to-date on news and events.

5. *Teen talk* – A number of schools and libraries have discovered that teens enjoy podcasting. In your school or library, you can give teens the chance to produce all aspects of a podcast: writing the outline or script, coming up with musical selections, recording, editing, and uploading.

6. *How-to* – Podcasts can be used for instruction on topics like how to find materials in the library, use technology, and find resources on a particular topic. These types of podcasts give listeners the chance to learn on their own time.

7. *Advocacy* – Use podcasts as a way to provide education on timely topics. For example, if your community has a school- or library-funding referendum on the ballot, create regular podcasts that explain to community members why it's important to have this money made available.

8. *Tours* – Give listeners an inside look at the school or library by providing behind-the-scenes tours of the facility. These, of course, work best as vidcasts, in which images of the location are integrated with the audio tour.

9. *Local history* – Dig into the history of your community by producing podcasts that inform listeners of the people, places, and events that make up the history of the city or town and/or highlight the local history resources available in the school or library.

10. *Who we are* – Putting a human face on school faculty and librarians can be a powerful way to gain support. Produce a podcast that introduces listeners to the people who work in your school or your library. Instead of simply talking about what the library or school offers, focus on the stories of the people who work in these institutions. What do they like to read? What do they like about their jobs? Who are they, really?

As you plan podcasts, consider the following:

Purpose

Start by asking yourself: "Why are we going to produce a podcast?" The 10 items at the beginning of this chapter give you an idea of what your goals for the podcast might be, and the sidebar beginning on page 15 highlights some popular options. Think about which ones best fit your abilities and your community. When you know what you are trying to accomplish with your podcast, you will be able to move forward with a clearer picture of the areas you need to focus on as you produce the audio (or video) files.

Audience

Who is your podcast going to be for? Will it be for anyone in the community? Will it be for a specific age group? Will it cover a specific topic area or subject matter? Knowing the group you are going to gear the podcast toward will be helpful as you make decisions about style and content.

Content

Once you have a good idea of the purpose and intended audience of your podcast, it should be much easier to decide on the content for the production. You may, for example, choose to gear the podcast to faculty members in order to inform them about library programs and services. Knowing this allows you to determine the content that specifically fits that audience and goal.

Buy-in

In most institutions, whenever a new project is in the works, it's important to get buy-in from groups ranging from other staff members to administrators. In your institution, make sure that you think about those in your organization who need to buy into the podcast project and figure out ways you can get that buy-in. One way to do this is by letting each individual know about a podcast they might listen to that would meet one of their personal needs or interests. For example, there may be a new mother on the staff who you would like to see buy into the project. Point her to MommyCast (www.mommycast.com) so she gets to see the benefit of podcasting as an informational tool. Or, maybe someone on the staff is a big fan of the TV show *Lost*. Point that person in the direction of the official *Lost* podcast (abc.go.com/primetime/lost/podcast).

Permissions and Consent

Make sure to consider whether you will need to develop permission forms for any of the podcast content you create. For example, if you intend to have minors participate in on-air podcast production, you'll need to get parental permission before you publish that content on the Web. If you create podcasts from presentations that take place at the library, you will want to make sure the speaker(s) provide permission for their presentation to be recorded and published via podcast.

Production Team

Who in the institution will work on the production of the podcast files? Will different people be responsible for different aspects of the production? For example, will one person be responsible for managing the recording, another person serve as the on-air talent, and someone else do the sound editing, or will one person play multiple roles? Also, decide if you are going to involve members of the community in the creation of the podcast content. If so, how will you get them involved? Will they need training before they participate in the production?

Technology Requirements

Make sure to plan for the technology you will need to produce successful podcasts. Think about which recording device you will use and about the software you will need to use to edit the files. (See Chapter 5 for more on recording and editing and suggestions of specific hardware and software.) Also, consider how much server space you need to have in order to upload the files to the Web and make them available for your audience to access. Don't forget that you'll need to create an RSS feed so that people are able to subscribe to the podcast. Will you create the feed on your own, or use a free service such as PodServe to do this for you?

Format

There are a couple of factors to consider when it comes to format. These factors include whether you are going to create a video or audio-only production, as well as the actual file format in which you make the podcast available. Think again about the audience and purpose of the cast. Determine whether video is necessary for the content you are going to provide. Think about whether the audience you are targeting has access to portable video devices and/or computer screens at the times you think they will be listening or viewing.

When it comes to the specific file format, download speeds, devices, and players are the key elements to consider. You will want to know what kinds of devices that your target podcast audiences will be using, as well as the type of connections they have, before you decide on a file format. You can read more about file formats in Chapter 5.

Training

Will the people involved in the production of the podcasts need any kind of training? Does someone need to know how to use the editing software? Does someone need to learn how to compress audio files? If training will be necessary, think about how you are going to make sure that those involved get the training or information they need.

Frequency

What are your goals in terms of the frequency of your podcast? Maybe your production team can produce an episode every month. Maybe the team can produce an episode every week. Here, you need to plan ahead. Remember, you want to create a podcast that people look forward to, and you want to stick to a regular schedule. You will want a new episode of the podcast to appear in listeners' podcatchers on a regular basis.

Length

The rule of thumb for podcasts is that they should be no longer than a traditional commute or recreational walk. Forty minutes can be a good amount of time, although some podcasts are, of course, longer than that and some are shorter. You can get a lot of content into an audio or video file in just three, five, or even 10 minutes. Think about when and how you expect your target audience will be listening to your production and then decide what timeframe works within that context. Remember, there's nothing wrong with only being able to listen to a portion of a file and then returning to it later. However, the content has to be compelling in order for someone to come back.

Marketing

Just because you create the podcast doesn't mean you will automatically have a built-in audience who will know about it, subscribe, and listen. Before you produce and launch your podcast, think about the ways you can market it to your target audience. A link on the institution's Web site is a good start, but what are some other ways you can get the word out? Are other podcasters that your target audience listens to willing to mention your new podcast? Can you get a mention on iTunes? What about sending information to listeners via text message or e-mail? Think outside of the box when it comes to getting the word out about your podcast. (See Chapter 6 for more on marketing your podcast.)

Put It in Writing

As you plan for your podcast launch, think about which aspects of the planning need to be put in writing in the form of policies, procedures, or a podcasting manual. Make sure to document the planning process thoroughly so that those who work with you and come after you can use the manual to keep the project going. This may even be the perfect opportunity to start a wiki for your organization, so that all of the planning, decision making, and policy development is available in a collaborative format.

Don't Feel Overwhelmed

Reading the reasons for podcasting and thinking about the planning that goes into each podcast might make you want to run for the hills; it does seem like a lot to actually think about and make happen. If you feel overwhelmed, though, remember the homegrown nature and roots of podcasts. While you do need to do some planning, the production you work on will also be different from the high-end production of a major media conglomerate—and that's a good thing! Take the time to plan first, so that you make sure you know what you want to accomplish and know how you will accomplish it. But, also leave yourself room to learn as you produce and be open to making changes as you go along. Start with your beginning ideas and let yourself be flexible when you learn how things really work. A plan can be changed. Goals can be rewritten. Start and see what happens.

Endnotes

1. Meg Canada (Web services librarian, Hennepin County Library, Minnetonka, Minnesota), online interview, August 2006.
2. Chris Kretz (digital resources librarian, Dowling College, Oakdale, New York), online interview, August 2006.

CHAPTER 3

Real Life Examples

One of the best ways to decide what you want to do with your own podcast is to spend some time listening to lots of different types of podcasts. These include both those created by institutions like your own and those created by people and organizations not at all like you. This chapter gives you a starting point for listening to and viewing podcasts from schools, libraries, regular old human beings, mainstream media, and other sources. This is not meant to be an all-encompassing list, a "what's hot" list, or the most up-to-date list. Instead, the following suggestions highlight a variety of podcasts that incorporate several different features you might consider as you work on your own podcast.

Also think about using podcasts for professional development. Do you have time to listen during your morning commute? At your desk? While making dinner? The sidebar on page 25 lists some useful podcasts for librarians.

Learning from Others

As you listen to podcasts, take note of what you like most about what you listen to and what you like the least. Use this information as you create your own podcasts, so you can replicate the good—and avoid duplicating the bad.

Please note that some podcasts have more than one subscription URL. (See Chapter 1 for information on subscribing to podcasts using iTunes or another podcatcher.) Don't forget that most of the podcasts listed also have a companion Web site, sometimes referred to as the "show notes." These provide more information on each podcast, links to resources discussed in a podcast, and opportunities to give feedback on podcast content. (See Chapter 4 for more information on podcast companion Web sites.)

Using OPML to Find and Exchange Podcasts

You can export your podcast subscription list as an OPML (Outline Processor Markup Language) file and make that file available to friends, colleagues, and people who listen to your podcast. Exchanging OPML files with others is a good way to find new podcasts that may be useful or entertaining, and a good way to get the word out about your own podcast. (Make sure that your podcast is listed as a subscription in your own OPML file!)

In most podcatchers, you'll find an export feature in the file menu of the software. When you click on "Export" in the file menu, a window opens that allows you to name the file, decide where you are going to save it, and select the file format. Make sure to select OPML.

Once your OPML subscription file is saved, you can exchange it with friends, colleagues, and podcast listeners by uploading the file to your server and then adding a link to it from your podcast's companion Web page. Others can then right-click (or ctrl-click on a Mac) on the link and select the "Save File" option in order to download it to their computer.

To import other people's OPML files into your podcatcher, first download and save the file to your computer. Then, select the "Import" link from the file menu of the podcatcher. A window will open and prompt you to navigate to where you wish to save the OPML file that you are importing.

You can test out importing a podcast subscription list into your podcatcher by using the OPML for the podcasts that I listen to. Go to www.leonline.com/listen_up/ and follow the steps to download the link titled "OPML file" to your computer.

Podcasts for Librarians

Podcasts about the world of librarianship are useful tools for professional development. These include:

- Library Geeks, onebiglibrary.net/geeks/ – The host of Library Geeks discusses a variety of topics related to technology in libraries. Past conversations have covered FRBR, the OpenOffice standard, and conferences of interest. These podcasts are all about software for libraries and just right for anyone who wants to know more about that topic.
- Library Luminary Lectures, senna.sjsu.edu/dfaires/blogs/luminaries/wordpress/ – The American Library Association Student Chapter at San Jose State University sponsors these podcasts, which are recordings of lectures at the university. Those wanting to learn more about a variety of topics related to librarianship and library education will find what they need with Library Luminary Lectures.
- LibVibe, libvibe.blogspot.com – Find out about current news in the library world via LibVibe. Episodes are produced approximately twice per week and cover a variety of library news topics, from successful programming to staff layoffs.
- LiSRadio, lisradio.missouri.edu/index.php – An abundance of library podcasts are available through LiSRadio. Productions include monthly interviews with readers and writers, a monthly show highlighting innovative things librarians are doing on the job, and discussions on the topic of human interaction behavior. This series not only provides relevant information to librarians about the field, it also serves as a good example of how an institution can build its own podcasting broadcast network.
- Talking with Talis, talk.talis.com – Listen to the Talking with Talis podcasts to learn about current and emerging trends and technologies in libraries. Productions include the Library 2.0 series (a roundtable discussion with librarians talking about library trends) and the Future Librarians Gang (a roundtable discussion with young librarians new to the field talking about what they see in store for libraries in the coming years).

Public Library

Cheshire (CT) Public Library
Podcast Web site: www.cheshirelib.org/teens/cplpodcast.htm
Subscription URL: feeds.feedburner.com/blogspot/Bfgf

The library's Web page for the podcast states: "The Cheshire Public Library Podcast is a teen-driven cultural magazine featuring teen writers, musicians, reviewers, commentators, and more." The approximately once-per-month podcast is entirely created and produced by teens. One or two hosts introduce each podcast and the segments within. The teens obviously have fun as they produce the audio files, and it's this fun that will bring listeners back to the podcast. You'll no doubt notice that the audio quality of the podcast varies from segment to segment, but that's not necessarily a detriment. This shows that the cast is homegrown, and it actually helps draw attention to the different segments.

Hennepin County Library, Minnetonka, Minnesota
Podcast Web site: www.hclib.org/teens/Podcasts.cfm
Subscription URL: hzapps.hclib.org/teens/Podcasts/GetXML.cfm

Each short (less than four minutes) podcast from the Hennepin County Library focuses on a specific content area. For example, a teen named Michael might talk about boys' reading and the library's book discussion group for boys. In separate podcasts, girls review various books and videos that interest them. There's also a podcast in which two teens talk about the library's international teen club. These podcasts demonstrate that short can be positive; the teens pack a lot of content into each episode.

Kankakee (IL) Public Library
Podcast Web site: www.lions-online.org/Podcasts.html
Subscription URL: www.lions-online.org/podcast.xml

See the sidebar interview with Kankakee Public Library Assistant Director Stephen Bertrand on page 27.

An Interview with Stephen Bertrand, Kankakee Public Library[1]

Q: How would you describe the content of your podcasts?
A: The majority of our podcasts are recordings of author talks held at the library. We do have one phone interview with Sue Monk Kidd and a teen poetry slam. We are looking into doing more interviews.

Q: When did Kankakee Public Library begin podcasting?
A: Our first podcast went online November 10, 2005. It was audio lifted from a video we made of a presentation by a survivor of the Dresden bombing. The first podcast recorded exclusively for that purpose was on December 8, 2005, when singer Arlo Guthrie visited our library.

Q: Why did your institution decide to start podcasting?
A: At the end of 2005 I purchased a new video iPod and started enjoying the podcasts I downloaded from iTunes. I did some investigating into what would be involved in podcasting our library programs. I was surprised to learn that we already had all the equipment needed to do the podcast: a laptop, a mixing board and microphones from our PA system, audio mixing software, and technical know-how. It was a pretty simple matter to capture the audio from the PA system during the talk into the laptop as an MP3. Since podcasting presented little to no additional cost, it was logical to give it a try.

Q: What type of guidelines did your institution create or put in place when you started podcasting?
A: The only requirement we have concerning our podcast is that we get permission from the speaker beforehand to be podcasted. Of the 10 or so podcasts we've produced, only one speaker has denied permission.

Q: What equipment do you use to record and produce your podcasts?
A: We use a Toshiba laptop connected to a Crate soundboard. We use a program called Super MP3 Recorder. The soundboard receives

the audio from the microphone and sends it to both the speakers for the public in attendance and to the laptop for the podcast recording. We then use Nero Wave Editor to edit the podcast. We just purchased a copy of Adobe Encore and intend to use that for recording and editing.

Q: If asked by a skeptical librarian, teacher, faculty member, or administrator what the benefits of podcasting are, what would you say?
A: I would tell them that the podcast allows our services to reach individuals not only in our normal service area of 27,000 people, but all over the world. Approximately 200 to 400 people attend each of our programs, while hundreds, even thousands more, hear them via our podcast. We have also garnered extensive public attention via our podcast. Noted author Luis Urrea even wrote an op-ed piece in the *New York Times* about us after being on one of our podcasts.

Q: What barriers do you find, if any, in order to be successful in podcasting at your institution?
A: I have no institutional barriers to our podcast. Our library board and administration are very supportive.

Q: What words of advice do you have for librarians, teachers, administrators, and faculty members who are interested in getting started with podcasting at their institution?
A: My biggest piece of advice would be to not think too locally. A podcast is a worldwide medium. Try to think of content that has interest to your local area, but also would be interesting to people outside your local area. What insights do you have locally that would be interesting globally?

Q: Is there anything else you think would be useful for librarians and educators to know about getting started in podcasting?
A: Podcasting is not as hard as it may seem initially. Many Web sites have clear directions on how to set up and produce one. All it takes is creativity and will. It is a way to make a very big splash with very little money. One little caution: Be careful of copyright. Get permission from speakers and artists. You can't just slap your favorite Beatles song into the podcast.

K–12

Coulee Kids Podcast, Longfellow Middle School, LaCrosse, Wisconsin

Podcast Web site: www.sdlax.net/longfellow/sc/ck/index.htm
Subscription URL: phobos.apple.com/WebObjects/MZStore.woa/wa/viewPodcast?id=79169064&s=143441

Longfellow Middle School teacher Jeanne Halderson introduced year two of the Coulee Kids podcasts by discussing the benefits of podcasting with middle school students. This overview is a perfect rundown of why student involvement in podcasting is a positive way to improve teaching and learning. Listen to the overview podcast to get ideas on how to start small and grow a podcast, and for ideas on how to sell podcasting to the community in which you work. Remember, this includes both your internal and your external community.

Radio WillowWeb, Willowdale Elementary School, Omaha, Nebraska

Podcast Web site: www.mpsomaha.org/willow/radio/
Subscription URL: feeds.feedburner.com/RadioWillowWeb

Produced periodically throughout the school year, Radio WillowWeb gives Willowdale Elementary School students the chance to talk about topics they are studying. Podcasts are between five and 15 minutes and feature short segments, including vocabulary related to the theme of the podcast, reports, poetry, interviews, reviews, and more. Highlights include the complete integration of student hosts for each episode (no adults are heard) and the use of sound effects and music that suit each theme perfectly.

College/University

Dowling College, Oakdale, New York

Podcast Web site: www.dowling.edu/library/newsblog/podcasts.asp
Subscription URL: www.dowling.edu/library/new/feed.xml

See the sidebar interview with Chris Kretz, digital resources librarian, Dowling College, on page 30.

An Interview with Chris Kretz, Dowling College[2]

Q: How would you describe the content of your podcasts?
A: We have a monthly podcast called Omnibus that is, as the name implies, a mixed bag of content (all of which is specifically created for the podcast). The bulk of it has been interviews with faculty, staff, librarians, and others on campus. The topics range from new developments at the library to specific classes, to ongoing research interests, to events on campus. We have also made a concentrated effort to cover local history, talking with neighboring historical societies, civic groups, and collectors. A smaller percentage of the content is scripted dramas built around our special collections on topics related to the area and the college. Many of the podcasts are designed to tie in with a "live" event, either a speaker on campus, a display in the library, or a community event.

Q: When did Dowling College begin podcasting?
A. Planning began in August 2005, and the first podcast was posted October 13, 2005.

Q. Why did your institution decide to start podcasting?
A. As a way to promote the library and its activities in a new and exciting way.

Q. What type of guidelines did your institution create or put in place when you started podcasting?
A. While there were no written guidelines, I did initially map out possible topics based on the life of the library. It quickly became apparent that possible topics were easily identified. Most podcasts can be tied back to a library collection, activity, or information literacy theme. Other general guidelines were to include as many different voices as possible and to try and tell a story (as opposed to just recite information available in other formats). The hope was to put the library in context, not just be descriptive about holdings,

hours, etc. Most of these guidelines have been broken at one point or another.

From listening to other podcasts, a general length of 15–20 minutes was the rule. Recordings were made at 44.1 khz, 16-bit mono to keep CD-quality sound. In terms of frequency, we have kept to a monthly schedule mostly to give enough time for production (the podcast is still mostly a one-man operation within the library). The audio quality is the best we can make it given our current equipment. Each podcast is carefully edited and previewed before posting.

Also from the beginning, the show notes have been a key part of the final product. The Web page/blog associated with our podcasts includes detailed information on each show as well as links to items in our collection and related material online.

Q. What equipment do you use to record and produce your podcasts?
A. Currently we use a Logitech USB microphone and record directly to a laptop or desktop computer running Audacity.

Q. If asked by a skeptical librarian, teacher, faculty member, or administrator what the benefits of podcasting are, what would you say?
A. Podcasting is a great opportunity to get information out to the community in a coherent, targeted, and engaging way.

Q. What barriers do you find, if any, in order to be successful in podcasting at your institution?
A. I think the greatest barrier is in promotion, raising awareness on campus. Why should anyone show any more interest in a library podcast than they do, say, in a library workshop. And although podcasting is becoming more a part of the cultural landscape, it does require effort on the part of the listener—to locate, download, and listen to each show. It has to be worthwhile for them to do it. What they hear has to be something they aren't hearing anywhere else.

Q. What words of advice do you have for librarians, teachers, administrators, and faculty members who are interested in getting started with podcasting at their institutions?
A. Listen to podcasts. Map out your ideas before recording. Check for any possible help with the audio end (IT, AV departments, etc). Be creative and tailor your content to your particular situation. Don't expect overnight results, persistence pays off.

Q. Is there anything else you think would be useful for librarians and educators to know about getting started in podcasting?
A. It takes time and effort (more than you think) but it is also an extremely rewarding experience.

Podcast for Teachers, Fordham University, Bronx, New York
Podcast Web site: www.podcastforteachers.org
Subscription URL: www.feedblitz.com/f/?Sub=50046

Two faculty members at Fordham University discuss a variety of topics related to education, including integrating technology into the classroom, recent education news, and teaching trends and techniques. A highlight of the podcast is the informal banter between the podcast hosts. The two hosts seem to enjoy each other's company and respect one another's views and opinions; they interact in an informal, joking manner that creates an entertaining and comfortable atmosphere for the listener. While this is an educational podcast, it contains no lecturing or formal classroom format.

Mainstream Media

***New York Times*: David Pogue**
Podcast Web site: www.nytimes.com/ref/multimedia/podcasts.html#pogue
Subscription URL: www.nytimes.com/services/xml/rss/nyt/podcasts/pogue.xml

In this weekly podcast, David Pogue reads his latest *New York Times* column. In one of his first podcasts, Pogue told his readers why he chose to simply read his column as opposed to creating entirely new audio content.[3] He noted that several listeners had e-mailed him to say they were disappointed that the podcast didn't include anything beyond what they could already read in the paper. Pogue's response was that he didn't have time to add yet another new production to his already busy weekly schedule. The podcast works well for people who don't have the time or inclination to read the print article, but prefer to listen. It's an audio version of text, something like an audio book (except, of course, much shorter). Pogue does a very good job of bringing his words to life, which is a highlight of this podcast; the reader's technique definitely makes a difference.

On the Media

Podcast Web site: www.onthemedia.org
Subscription URL: feeds.wnyc.org/onthemedia

In this podcast version of the weekly National Public Radio program, listeners get to listen to each On the Media program at a time that is convenient for them. The highlight of the podcast version is the example it provides of taking content produced originally for another medium and repurposing it slightly for the podcasting format.

***TV Guide* Talk**

Podcast Web site: www.tvguide.com/news/podcast
Subscription URL: www.tvguide.com/news/podcast/rss.xml

Listeners of *TV Guide* Talk get to hear the magazine's writers talk about entertainment news and gossip. This is another example of a podcast that uses an informal format to provide information to listeners. There is a lot of joking among the staffers, and the way the podcast is produced gives listeners the sense that the hosts are just hanging out with each other and talking about entertainment topics. This informality within a mainstream media production is a definite highlight of the podcast.

Homegrown

Ask a Ninja

Podcast Web site: www.askaninja.com
Subscription URL: phobos.apple.com/WebObjects/MZFinance.woa/wa/subscribePodcast?id=115933673

Ask a Ninja is a vidcast that is just plain silly and fun to watch. Each episode presents a ninja answering a question sent in by a viewer, in honest ninja fashion. The hallmark of this podcast is its humor and simplicity. Even a talking head in front of a red backdrop can be interesting to watch when well scripted.

Coverville
Podcast Web site: coverville.com
Subscription URL: feeds.feedburner.com/coverville/

Three times a week, Coverville host Brian Ibbott produces a podcast all about cover music. Each installment is theme-based, from Woodstock, to Depeche Mode, to the Ramones, to the Ides of March. Ibbott does a good job with his hosting duties, moving from the songs to information about the covers and the originals from which they sprang. Highlights of this podcast include its ability to take a traditional radio form and make it work within the podcast format. It's also important to note that, in order to play the full songs on Coverville, Ibbott pays royalties to ASCAP/BMI. Read about Ibbott's license at the Podcast Alley forums (www.podcastalley.com/forum/showthread.php?t=120612).

Daily SearchCast
Podcast Web site: dailysearchcast.com
Subscription URL: afeeds.daggle.com/scast/

Daily SearchCast covers the latest news in the Web search world, as an audio companion to the popular Web site Search Engine Watch (www.searchenginewatch.com). It might be hard to believe that search engine news could be entertaining—and even funny at times—but the hosts of Daily SearchCast actually pull it off. In between news about Yahoo!, Google, and other search tools, the hosts of the podcast talk about their lives and about the Web world in general. The Daily SearchCast is also a good example of a podcast that is produced when the hosts are in two different locations. Daily SearchCast hosts use VoIP (Voice Over Internet Protocol) to talk to each other. This demonstrates that podcast hosts and guests do not have to sit in the same room in order to participate in the same podcast. (See Chapter 4 for more on VoIP podcasting.)

Daily Source Code
Podcast Web site: www.dailysourcecode.com
Subscription URL: www.podshow.com/feeds/dailysourcecode. xml

Adam Curry, known as one of the fathers of podcasting, is the host of the Daily Source Code. Anyone just learning about podcasting would do well to listen to Curry's production. This is a good way to find out what's going on in the podcast world and to learn how a one-person show can keep people interested. Another highlight of the podcast is its integration of clips from other podcasts, which is a great way to advertise podcast content.

Diggnation

Podcast Web site: revision3.com/diggnation

Subscription URL (video version): revision3.com/diggnation/feed/small.mov.xml

Subscription URL (audio version): revision3.com/diggnation/feed/high.mp3.torrent.xml

Imagine two former frat boys in their early 30s sitting on a couch with their computers, drinking beer, and talking about technology news. That's what you get with both the video and audio versions of Diggnation. This podcast is a good way to find out about the latest news in technology from people inside the technology world. The two hosts are entertaining commentators on the world of tech—and the world at large. This, once again, is a good example of how informality in a podcast works successfully.

Rocketboom

Podcast Web site: www.rocketboom.com/vlog/

Subscription URL: www.rocketboom.com/vlog/rss.html

This daily vidcast is a pseudo-newscast that covers odd (and not so odd) news in a humorous fashion. The female host sits at a traditional news desk, but reads nontraditional stories. This is a good example of taking a traditional style of video production and content and changing it for the podcasting world. (Think John Stewart and Steven Colbert for the podcast set.)

TWiT (This Week in Tech)

Podcast Web site: www.twit.tv/twit

Subscription URL: leoville.tv/podcasts/twit.xml

One of the podcasts created as a part of the TWiT family of productions, TWiT is a weekly roundtable made up of four or five technology pundits talking about the latest technology news. In most cases, each participant is in a different location—so this is another example of a podcast that uses VoIP technology. The group has a set list of topics they plan to talk about during each weekly production; they do at times, though, go off on interesting tangents.

What These Podcasts Teach Us

The next two chapters go into detail about what makes a good podcast from two major angles—content and production techniques. However, it's apparent from the podcasts described in this chapter that the primary selling point for many is their homemade, informal format and the atmosphere that the podcast producers create. The very informality of many of these casts draws the listener or viewer in. Remember this as you read the next chapters and begin to work on your own podcasts.

Endnotes

1. Stephen Bertrand (assistant director, Kankakee (IL) Public Library), online interview, August 2006.
2. Chris Kretz (digital resources librarian, Dowling College, New York), online interview, August 2006.
3. David Pogue, *New York Times*: David Pogue (New York Times Co., June 1, 2006), 10 min. 17 sec. podcast, odeo.com/channel/104368/view/2 (accessed November 26, 2006).

CHAPTER 4

What Makes a Great Podcast? Developing the Content

Chapter 2 discussed the importance of deciding on your reasons for creating a podcast before going into production. Once you have determined your purpose, goals, and audience, you should then make some decisions about the format, organization, and content of your podcast.

Formal vs. Informal

When planning the content of your podcasts—whether the first or 30th installment—it's important to determine if you are going to use a formal or informal approach. A formal presentation is tightly scripted, without much diversion from the overall plan. One example of a scripted podcast is David Pogue reading his *New York Times* column during his weekly technology podcast (described in Chapter 3). Another example of a scripted podcast is one in which the on-air talent reads directly from printed reviews of books or other written works.

Of course, even tightly scripted podcasts can sound informal—or interesting. In such cases, the informality comes from the reader's style. Even though Pogue, for instance, reads directly from his column, he uses pacing and inflection to make the reading interesting. The recording doesn't come off as staid and boring; it's very much like listening to a theater production or an audiobook performance. Ultimately, even those podcasters who use a tightly scripted format want to work toward sounding informal and conversational as they read the scripts they have prepared.

When working from an outline, as opposed to a full script, the podcaster doesn't read her content word-for-word. She does, however, have ideas (and perhaps annotations for those ideas) written out ahead of time. She creates her podcast from that list and annotations. You may create different forms of outlines for different forms of podcasts. For example:

- A podcast about current news and trends in technology might simply use a list of annotated links as the outline for the production. An example of this is the TWiT podcast. The guests on the show have access to links saved to del.icio.us (del.icio.us/twit), and that set of links acts as the outline for the podcast. As the conversation takes place, the guests and hosts look through the links list and bring up topics to discuss.
- On the Cranky Geeks vidcast (www.crankygeeks.com), host John C. Dvorak works from a set of notecards with information about the topics the panelists on the show are discussing. This vidcast is a roundtable forum, and the formal aspect of the show stems from the set list of topics discussed, its informal nature from the way the panelists discuss each topic.
- For a podcast I record for students enrolled in a class I teach, I first make an outline listing the topics I want to cover, which relate to the theme of the week's class. I sometimes make notes about points I want to make within a topic, but often, I simply list the topics and speak extemporaneously using my own experience and knowledge to feed the conversation.

Podcast outlines help guarantee that the topics that need to be covered are covered. But, when only using an outline instead of a full script, the podcaster needs to have a strong knowledge of the topic in order to speak about it coherently and effectively. Some podcasters find that as they are first getting used to the technology of podcasting they like to start by working from full scripts. That way, podcasters don't have to rely quite so heavily on their own understanding of a topic. When they become more comfortable with the way podcasting works, podcasters can move on to speaking from an outline. Their first outlines might be pretty complete—almost like a script—but, over time, these outlines can become less comprehensive and provide more opportunities for off-the-cuff conversation.

Formal Introductions and Closings

Whether a podcast is fully scripted or outlined, it's a good idea to use a formal opening and closing that tells listeners which podcast they are listening to and introduces the content of the current installment. For example, the theme song to the Daily Giz Wiz (gizwiz.biz) is always the same. I know what to expect when I hear that theme. After the theme plays, I know that the host, Leo Laporte, is going to let listeners know what the gadget of the day is.

Similarly, at the end of the Daily Giz Wiz, the co-hosts always close with the same tag lines and play the theme song again. I know when I hear those tag lines that the podcast is just about over, and when the theme song plays, I know that the production has ended.

When podcasters use a formal introduction and closing, the listener is given a complete package. Even if the podcast itself is very informal, adding an opening and closing that stay the same from installment to installment helps put people in the mood to listen, provides an alert of what's to come, and gives a sense of completeness to what was just heard.

In Podcast for Teachers, described in Chapter 3, the hosts vocally introduce the podcast the same way from week to week, but the opening and closing music for each week's production is different. Dr. Kathy King, one of the podcast's hosts, once remarked that she varies the music in order to give listeners the chance to hear lots of different music available for inclusion in podcasts.[1] That makes sense for her audience, which is made up of educators who are learning about technology and about how to podcast. However, as a podcast producer, you will want to consider this carefully. Decide if it's better to have a consistent theme song for the opening and closing that acts as a connection between your listeners and your podcast, or if it's better to vary the music in order to expand listeners' horizons.

Music for Podcasts

In his sidebar interview in Chapter 3, Stephen Bertrand noted that podcasters need to be careful about the music they use. As he remarked, just because a Beatles song would provide the right feeling for a podcast, that doesn't mean a podcaster has the right to use that song.

There are many places to obtain music for use in podcasts that is free of traditional copyright restrictions. Some of the first podcasters were musicians who used podcasting as a way to get their music out to the world. Musicians are still making their music freely available for use in podcasts.

In most cases, sites that provide music for use in podcasts do require registration, and the registration process asks for the URL of the podcast in which the music will be used. This, of course, means that you need to have a host for your podcast before you begin downloading music. (See Chapter 5 for information on setting up a podcast host.) Once you sign up for a podcast music service, you can save the music that interests you to your account, download the music in MP3 format, and add either clips or full songs to your podcasts. Usually the music site will request that you let them know when you use one of their songs so that the musicians can be informed about where their music is being played.

Providers of music for podcasts include:

- IODA Promonet, promonet.iodalliance.com/login.php
- Magnatune, magnatune.com/info/podcast
- Podsafe Audio, www.podsafeaudio.com
- Podsafe Music Network, music.podshow.com

The music available on these sites is often licensed through Creative Commons. The Creative Commons Web site includes some useful information on legal issues that podcasters need to be aware of, and the Podcasting Legal Guide (wiki.creativecommons.org/podcasting_legal_guide/) at the Creative Commons site includes both a section on music and one on podcasting and copyright issues for librarians and teachers. You can also listen to a podcast produced by YALSA (Young Adult Library Services Association) about music for podcasts (pod-serve.com/audiofile/filename/4111/creative_commons_music.mp3).

Using Music in Podcasts

Using music at the beginning and end of a podcast is the perfect way to open and close each installment. Music can be used to good effect within a podcast as well. For example:

- If a podcast is made up of a series of segments, each segment might have a different style of music playing underneath in order to highlight its unique content. In a podcast produced for YALSA by teens at the Cheshire (CT) Public Library, each segment of the production has a different teen discussing the role technology plays in his or her life (blogs.ala.org/yalsa.php?title=yalsa_podcast_3_teens_talk_technology&more=1&c=1&tb=1&pb=1). Underneath each teen's comments, listeners hear a different style of music that relates to the information presented.

- If a podcast is made up of different segments, music can be inserted in between each segment in order to separate the content. For example, a podcast that focuses on a series of book reviews might include a musical interlude in between reviews on different genres of books—mystery, realism, fantasy, and so on—to alert the listener that the genre up for discussion is changing.
- In a podcast interview, if the discussion jumps from one topic to another, music can be used to help connect the sections of the podcast. For example, in an interview with an author, music might be used as a transition between the author speaking about his childhood to a discussion of where the author finds inspiration for his work.
- A piece of music might be played quietly throughout an entire podcast to highlight its content. For example, in a podcast interview with an expert on the American Revolution, a military march might provide background sound to the entire production.

In Chapter 5, I talk about creating audio files and considering sound levels and quality. Remember, if you are going to use music in your podcast, either as a way to open and close the production or as part of the podcast content, it's important to balance the volume and levels of the music so that they support the spoken word without overwhelming it.

When deciding on what music to include in your podcast, don't forget that there might be local musicians in your community who can provide just what you need. Put out the word that you are looking for independent musicians to score your podcast production. By including the music of local artists, you help their careers and also help to create a unique, local feel.

Using Visuals in Vidcasts

The visuals on the Ask a Ninja podcast usually consist of a sheet hung on the wall and a man dressed up as a Ninja. In Diggnation, the viewer sees two guys sitting on a couch in one guy's apartment. In Cranky Geeks, the view is of three or four people sitting around a table. None of these popular podcasts features elaborate sets or extravagant visuals. The lack of glitz, though, is part of their appeal. The basic visuals stem from a desire to preserve the homemade quality of the production.

As you develop your vidcast, remember that your set doesn't have to be high-tech or elaborate. You might sit around a library office, on an information commons couch, in a classroom, or in the staff lounge, just talking about whatever your podcast covers. Don't worry about making everything look like network TV; focus on content over glitz.

Working with Others

When producing a podcast, don't feel like you have to go it all alone. There are many different ways in which you can podcast without being the lone voice of your institution. Consider the following possibilities for getting other people involved:

- *Get students and community members involved* – Imagine creating an oral history podcast where students are trained on how to interview community members. Students would be armed with recording devices and interviewing techniques, and would then be responsible for editing and producing the podcasts. Your role would be to manage the project and lend assistance as needed.
- *Work with colleagues to produce podcasts on a regular basis* – Especially in a public library system or consortium, a different librarian can take responsibility for each production. It would be important to make sure that the general focus of the podcast stayed the same from producer to producer, but, beyond that, each podcaster would be responsible for the specific content of his or her installment.
- *Hold training sessions for colleagues and students* – Let them learn how to create a podcast. When the training is

complete, offer to help trainees set up social podcasts related to specific themes of interest. By providing this training, you encourage local podcasting and guarantee that you get the message out about the role your school or library plays in the community.

A useful tool for working with others in podcast production is a Web-based calendar system. For example, it's possible to set up a group Google Calendar at calendar.google.com for those involved in a particular project. The participants can sign up on the calendar for the dates on which they will publish, distribute, and record, as well as sign up for specific areas of content on which they will focus. By using a tool of this kind, each participant can see the podcast schedule and uncover schedule and topic holes.

Show Notes

Managing podcast content with a calendar tool is one preproduction way of organizing and scheduling podcast content. Once the podcast is produced, and as it's distributed, it's also important to post information on the episodes on a companion Web site. Podcasters refer to postings on such a site as "show notes." These show notes list the topics included in a podcast and provide links to sites and content discussed.

The show notes not only give listeners a chance to see more information about the content that was discussed in a particular podcast installment, but the notes site itself also acts as an archive of each podcast and the topics discussed. Through the show notes, a listener can go back many months later to read about the content and find links of interest. Similarly, through the show notes, a searcher might find information about a podcast's content simply by running across the show notes Web site or via a Google search.

The Web site that hosts the show notes is also the place where listeners can find a link to subscribe to the podcast, download the podcast, or listen to a streamed version. (In a streamed version, listeners or viewers access the media file straight from the show notes Web site instead of first downloading it to their computer or portable device.)

Podcasters often use blogs as the home for their show notes. This is because blogging software makes it easy to create a feed for both podcasts and new blog posts. Blogs also make it easy for listeners to post comments about a particular podcast installment. PodOmatic (www.podamatic.com) is a Web service that makes it easy to upload podcast content and create a blog that acts as a show notes site.

You can read about show notes as a marketing tool for your podcast in Chapter 6.

Consistency Is Key

Once you determine a podcast's format and style, it's important to stick with that format and style. You want your listeners to learn to expect a certain type of podcast with a certain feel and framework. The feel comes from the way you integrate music into the production, the way you organize the content, and the formality or informality of the podcast.

Don't forget that a podcast should be produced on a regular schedule so that listeners know when to expect a new episode. You want listeners to look forward to the date when the next installment will come out, and you don't want to disappoint them too often by skipping a podcast. If for some reason you can't keep to the planned schedule, make sure to explain why. You can do that on your podcast show notes site, by producing a short podcast that informs subscribers about the glitch in the schedule, or during the next full podcast that you publish.

Similarly, the length of your podcast should not vary greatly from episode to episode. Decide up front how long each show will be and then stick with that general time frame. You don't have to know that each installment will be exactly 12 minutes and 12 seconds, but you should keep to a general time frame of, say, less than 10 minutes, or of 10 to 20 minutes. If there are times that the length of your podcast varies (which should be infrequent), let your listeners know in the introduction of the production and via the show notes. (Of course, the listener can discern from the file size approximately how long a podcast is, but it is still more audience-friendly to address the time change with listeners as a part of the episode.)

Podcasts are a great way to build interest in the work that you do as a teacher or librarian. It might be hard to keep up the momentum and continue to produce a podcast on a regular basis, but once you have listeners who start to give you feedback on the content you create, you'll probably find that the comments you receive help to keep you going. Don't forget to pay attention to what your listeners have to say and to keep them in the loop about your production.

Endnote

1. Dr. Kathy King and Mark Gura, Podcast for Teachers (PFT, October 23, 2006), 36 min. 40 sec. podcast, media.libsyn.com/media/retc/PFT_2_09_60_102306.mp3 (accessed November 27, 2006).

CHAPTER 5

What Makes a Great Podcast? The Technology

Teaching people how to create podcasts is one of my favorite things to do. Why? Because many people assume that creating podcasts is extremely difficult; they think that they have to have lots of equipment and technical knowledge. But within a very short period of time, sometimes as little as 30 minutes, they learn that anyone can produce a podcast. In most instances, the production can also be done for a very low cost.

In this chapter, you'll learn what it takes to create a podcast, including suggestions on the equipment and software to use for recording. You'll find out about editing software, learn about file formats, and gather some tips for making quality audio and video. This chapter is not intended to act as a complete guide to creating audio and video for podcasts. It will, however, provide you with a working knowledge of the types of technology to look for, hardware and software recommendations, and a set of tools to use to get started podcasting both audio and video. You can find links to more information on a number of podcasting tools in Appendix B.

Making the Recording

At its most basic, to record a podcast you need a recording device—a microphone or a video camera. If you are recording straight to the computer, you will also need software to save the audio or video. (Of course, you also need the talent, the people who will be heard or seen.)

Don't forget that it's possible to make a recording of people even when those people are in different locations. Many podcasters use VoIP (Voice Over Internet Protocol) technology to record participants in disparate locations. For example, on the TWiT podcast, the members of the weekly roundtable are often located in multiple locations around the U.S. or as far away as Great Britain. The guests use Skype (www.skype.com) to connect to each other via their computers and microphones, and these conversations are recorded and distributed as podcasts. (The host of TWiT, Leo Laporte, writes about how the show is recorded and produced on the TWiT Web site at www.twit.tv/podcastequipment.)

The fact that it's possible to record podcasts with people who aren't in the same location opens up many possibilities for libraries and schools. Librarians might interview an author across the country, or teachers might host a roundtable of colleagues from around the country to talk about pedagogy. If you do record using VoIP, you might need to use a different microphone than that used for single-person recordings. Laporte writes that "all participants are required to have headset microphones. ... USB headsets seem to perform better than others."[1] By insisting that guests have headsets, Laporte helps guarantee the recording is high quality. (For one thing, the use of headsets guarantees that listeners never hear reverb or echo in the recording.)

Another factor to consider when selecting the recording hardware for a podcast is whether recordings will be made straight onto a computer, or whether recordings will be made while you are away from your computer. For example, a librarian might decide to record man-on-the-street interviews to find out how members of the community feel about the library's plans to build a new facility. The librarian wouldn't bring her computer out onto the street. Instead, she would use a digital voice recorder (DVR) to capture the audio. When the librarian returns to her computer, she can connect the recorder to the computer, upload the files, and then either proceed with additional recording or start editing the files.

It is important to think about where recordings are going to be made when making podcast hardware decisions. The following section looks at a few hardware options and possible tools to use in recording podcasts.

Using Skype for VoIP

Skype is one of the most commonly used VoIP software programs. This free software gives users the chance to communicate using a computer and the Internet. Using Skype is like making a phone call, except you use speakers and a microphone instead of a telephone and handset.

To set up Skype, you need to:

- Download the software at www.skype.com
- Install the software
- Set up an account with a user name and password
- Add friends to your Skype contacts list

When any of the friends on your Skype contact list are available, you can tell by the green circle with a checkmark through it next to his or her user name. To call that person using Skype, you just double-click on his or her name, and you will hear your friend's computer start ringing. That friend will answer the call by clicking on a green headset icon in his or her Skype friends list, and then the two of you can start talking.

Skype also allows users to set up conference calls with up to five people (including the call host). This is a great way to set up roundtable-style podcasts.

Microphones

Many computers come with built-in microphones, or external microphones are packaged with the hardware. If your computer doesn't come with a microphone, you have several options for purchasing an external microphone that you can hook up to your computer. Even if your computer does come with a built-in microphone, you might want to purchase an external microphone in order to improve the quality of the recording. It's possible to pay as little as $5 for a microphone or as much as several hundred dollars. The quality of the recording varies greatly based on the quality of the microphone. (However, higher cost doesn't always equal better quality.) In most cases, podcasters in schools and libraries can create high-quality productions with inexpensive microphones that cost between $15 and

$60. If you do become a regular podcaster, you will likely want to upgrade your microphone beyond the $15 range.

In his book *Secrets of Podcasting: Audio Blogging for the Masses, 2nd edition,* Bart Farkas goes into detail about different microphone options, costs, and the pros and cons of various styles and manufacturers. Two microphones Farkas discusses include:

- *Labtec Desk Mic534* – The Labtec is a small lightweight microphone that is easy to find at most computer stores and doesn't have a high price tag. The microphone retails for $14.99 and is a great choice for beginning podcasters. The audio quality is decent, it's easy to use, and it has a mute feature. This is a good microphone for podcasts in which one or two people sit around a computer to record an episode's content.
- *Logitech USB Headset 250* – This Logitech headphone and microphone combination plugs into a USB port on a computer. This option provides a podcaster recording people in different locations a good, inexpensive ($39.99) way to hear and record voices from computer to computer.

Beyond microphones, when choosing a digital voice recorder for away-from-computer recordings, you might look at options such as:

- *Olympus VN 2100* – The Olympus VN 2100 digital voice recorder is small and lightweight. The interface is easy to use and the device allows for many hours of recording without filling up the hardware's memory or using up the battery life. The recording quality is good too. Its $60 price makes this a good DVR for beginning podcasters who want to see how this type of device works.

As mentioned previously, you have many options for recording devices. You can also purchase microphones that can be added to portable media devices such as an iPod. Some portable media devices have recording functionality, including a built-in microphone. Devices that come with built-in recording capabilities include the SanDisk Sansa e280 MP3 player and the iRiver Clix. It's a good idea for beginning podcasters to start with a microphone that's easy to use so that figuring out the use of the equipment doesn't become a barrier to making a recording.

Recording Audio

One of the first pieces of software many podcasters use when creating an audio podcast is Audacity (audacity.sourceforge.net). The use of Audacity is widespread partly because it is a free download. Its popularity, though, also stems from the fact that the software is very easy to use and provides tools for both recording and editing audio. Audacity is available for Windows and Mac computers.

Apple also sells a piece of Mac-only software called GarageBand (www.apple.com/ilife/garageband/) that can be used for making podcasts. GarageBand is part of the Mac iLife suite of products, which is bundled with new Macs or available for purchase for approximately $80. GarageBand has many of the same recording features as Audacity, plus two features that Audacity lacks: the ability to add an image to a podcast file, and the ability to create enhanced podcasts. In an enhanced podcast, the podcaster can add "chapters" to the recording. The chapter markings in a recording make it easier to find and skip to specific audio content. Currently, iPods are the only portable media devices that can take advantage of enhanced podcasts, although iTunes also provides the capability of moving from chapter to chapter when listening on a computer. Devices that don't support enhanced podcasting, though, can still play an enhanced podcast; the enhanced features are simply not available.

There are many other low-cost or no-cost products available for recording podcasts. These include Audio Hijack Pro (Mac only; www.rogueamoeba.com/audiohijack/) and Sound Recorder (Windows only; www.soundrecorder.net). Some plug-ins also allow for easy recording of Skype conversations. These include HotRecorder for Windows (www.hotrecorder.com) and Call Recorder for Mac (www.ecamm.com/mac/callrecorder/). However, if you have a program like Audacity on your computer, you can simply use it to record Skype calls. All you need to do is click the record button on the software and then start talking; it will pick up all sides of the conversation.

When recording, perform a few tests to make sure you get the highest audio quality possible. You don't want to record an entire podcast only to later find out in the playback that the sound didn't work the way you hoped. Start the recording session by testing the microphone and the audio levels to make sure they meet your needs. Some areas you want to pay attention to include:

- *Be aware of microphone placement* – Many podcasters think that they need to hold the microphone very close to their mouth, but that's not usually the case. The closer the microphone is to your mouth, the more likely it is that you'll pick up the extra sounds you make when you speak, for example, the popping of letters such as the letter "p" and the slur or hissing of the letter "s." In most cases, the microphone should be from five to six inches away from the mouth of the person who is speaking.

- *Watch the sound levels* – All recording software shows sound levels on a section of the screen. Pay attention to these, and make sure as you test the recording that you get sound levels that are going to make for a good listening experience. As Barrett Golding writes: "Get Good Levels. These meters are registering well: high enough (just into the red) to mask the noise (inherent in all recorders), but not too high (always in the red) as to make the recorder distort. Digital recorders (DAT, mini-disc, computer), compared to analog (cassette, reel), are much less noisy, but much more sensitive to distortion. When recording digitally, never max out your levels. ... If your meter has numbers, keep the peak levels between -6db and -12db."[2]
- *Record any ambient/atmospheric sound that you might want to use before you start recording the podcast content* – This can be helpful if you need to add silence to the podcast or if you need to add natural sound to the background of a portion of the podcast.
- *Realize that you can't edit out sounds in a recording if they are a part of the full audio* – For example, you might listen to your podcast after it's recorded and realize that you can hear the low hum of your computer fan in the background of the entire recording. Since the fan sound is a part of the background of the entire recording, you can't isolate it in order to remove it. The only way to delete that sound would be if you could capture it in the audio at a time when that was the only thing that could be heard.

Video Cameras

It's more and more common for computer hardware to come with a built-in camera. Some Mac and Windows computers have cameras installed inside their monitors. This makes it easy to make a one-person vidcast straight from a computer. These can also be used to capture video of people in different locations, just like Skype can be used to capture audio of people in different locations. (And, new versions of Skype record both audio and video.) An internal camera can therefore be used for either single-person or roundtable vidcast productions including people in a variety of locations.

Aside from using a built-in computer camera, vidcasters can also shoot video with an external video camera, upload the files to a computer, and then edit and produce the vidcast. Video cameras, of course, do cost more money than the microphones that were discussed previously. In most cases, you can purchase a low-end camera that produces decent video for about $300. More expensive cameras offer more recording features, and sometimes—but not always—better quality.

When selecting a video camera to use in podcasts, some features to consider include:

- *Ease of use* – Look for a camera you don't need to take a course on in order to use. Sometimes cameras that come with extra features require a steep learning curve. If this is your first experience with a video camera, then go with something simple; don't create unnecessary barriers to recording.
- *Computer transfer* – Pay attention to the method required for transferring files to a computer. Some cameras use USB connectors, and some use FireWire to make a connection between the camera and the computer. You want to make sure that your computer supports the connector used by the camera.
- *Sound recording* – You aren't just recording home movies. You want to make sure the camera does a good job recording sound as well as video so that subscribers to your vidcast can hear the production as well as they can see it. Consider purchasing a video camera that includes a jack for an external microphone so you have options when it comes to the way the audio is recorded.
- *Tripod* – In most cases, you aren't going to want to hold the video camera in your hands while recording, so purchase a tripod to set the camera on in order to make a stable

recording. A tripod may come bundled with the camera you want to purchase; even so, you should test out the included tripod to make sure it provides adequate stability. Also look for a tripod that allows you to move the camera around its axis.

Good video camera choices for beginners include:

- *Canon Elura 100* – This small camera takes good video images, except in low-light situations. It has on-board recording space, so you don't need anything extra in order to record and save your video.
- *Sanyo Xacti VPC-C40* – This is an inexpensive, small, lightweight digital camera that is good for those just getting started in video recording. This recorder uses an SD card to store recordings, so don't forget to buy one of those too.

Recording Video

If you are using a video camera to record video, you don't need to download recording software to your computer; the camera does all of the work. However, you do want to make sure of a few things whenever you record video:

- *Watch the lighting* – Emily Price writes: "Camcorders typically have a difficult time recording video in darker areas. Camcorders will typically make video shot in dim areas look as though it was shot in complete darkness."[3]
- *Don't overuse the zoom* – While it might seem like a good idea to go back and forth between close-ups and overview shots, zooming in and out too often will only annoy your viewers.
- *Keep it simple* – While the camera you are using might provide options for special effects, it's likely that the best video you can produce is one that simply focuses on the people doing the talking. If you want to add transitions and other effects, do this when you are editing the video.
- *Don't forget the tripod* – Make sure to use it to create a stable viewing experience for your audience.

Recording Screencasts

One other type of visual that can be used for distribution is called a "screencast." A screencast is a movie that records whatever is being displayed on a computer monitor. This technology is popular with educational institutions as a way to produce and distribute how-to's on everything from using the library catalog to a tour of the stacks of a library. More recent versions of screencast software also provide the capability to create portable-media-device-ready files, so screencasts can be produced in a format that will work on an iPod or any other portable media device that plays video.

Two software products currently dominate the screencast market, Adobe Captivate (www.adobe.com/products/captivate/) and Camtasia (www.techsmith.com/camtasia.asp). Each product has similar features, allowing video producers to record or import audio, add transitions, integrate live-motion video, and more. (As of May 2007, neither product was available for the Mac.)

Imagine if one of your library customers could watch a screencast showing her how to use the library catalog remotely. She can watch the video while she hunts for materials from the comfort of her dorm room. Or, she can download it to her portable media device and watch it as she rides the subway to work. Don't miss the opportunities screencasts provide to use podcasting technology to inform users how to use resources remotely—and in the palms of their hands.

Libraries currently using screencasting to reach their patrons include:

- Virginia Commonwealth University, Richmond, VA, Finding Journals in the Library (blog.vcu.edu/lse/2006/01/locating_a_journal_in_cabell_1.html) – One of the highlights of this screencast on how to access library journals is the integration of movies that actually show the library stacks. Students see the inside of the library, so they learn what the shelves look like and where journals are stored on library shelves.

- New York University, NY, Bobst Library, How to Find a Book (library.nyu.edu/research/tutorials/movie/book/) – This step-by-step tutorial on how to find materials using the university's library catalog integrates a menu system, so viewers can decide whether to watch the entire screencast or a specific portion of the tutorial.

Editing

One concept to remember when recording a podcast is that lots of things (not everything, but quite a bit) can be cleaned up in the editing process. Editing, however, is the step that takes the most time when producing a podcast. For every hour of podcast content you record, you will find—at least when you are starting out—that you spend two to four hours editing. That time does become shorter once you become familiar with the editing tools and how they work. But when you are starting out, do be prepared for many hours "in the editing room."

Editing Audio

While Audacity and GarageBand are the two most popular pieces of software for recording audio, both also allow you to edit audio. They include some very helpful features, such as:

- *Multiple tracks* – Both programs allow you to add tracks and to add different sections of audio on each track. For example, an audio file created with these software programs might include a track for the host of the episode, a track for the opening and closing music, a track for the audio of a guest on the podcast, and a track for the background music that plays underneath the speakers. The ability to put audio on different tracks is important, as it is easier to edit the different sections of audio when they are on separate tracks.
- *Cut, move, and trim* – While working with an audio recording, an editor can listen to the content and cut out any sections that aren't necessary, reorganize content in order to create a better flow, and trim off small portions of audio in order to make sure that the entire file has a seamless sound.
- *Volume enhancement* – If one portion of the audio is quieter than the other portions, these editing tools let an editor select the quiet portion and raise the volume to a level close to that of the other sections of the recording.
- *Special effects* – Both pieces of software provide features allowing you to change the sound of the audio in order to enhance a special effect. In Audacity, you can use the feature to insert silence, create vocal sounds (such as

"wah-wah"), and clean up any background noise that might interfere with the quality of the recording. In GarageBand, it's possible to add vocal effects such as echo and reverb, among other options provided by the software.

- *Zoom* – Each software program makes it possible to zoom into the recording in order to select the exact section with which you want to work. This is important, since without this feature, it's impossible to guarantee that you will be able to select the exact piece of audio that you want to cut, move, trim, or work with.
- *Audio import* – This is what makes it possible to add music to an audio file being edited in Audacity or GarageBand. This is also the way that audio editors can combine audio files recorded at different times.

For beginning podcasters, Audacity and GarageBand have all the necessary features for creating audio for podcasts. Other software may have more advanced features, but most of these "extras" are not required when creating a homegrown library or school podcast.

If you are using a DVR that saves files in a format such as WAV or WMA that is not recognized by Audacity or GarageBand, you can convert those files to MP3 format with another program, such as iTunes. To convert a file with iTunes, you import it into your iTunes library, select it in your library listing, and select "Advanced ...", then "Convert to MP3." Once the file is in MP3 format, you can import it into Audacity or GarageBand and edit it just as you would a file that you originally recorded with one of these software programs.

Editing Video

Two low-cost products are available for editing video, the Windows-only Adobe Premiere Elements (the "light" version of Adobe Premiere; www.adobe.com/products/premiereel/) and the Mac-only iMovie (Apple's iLife product for movie editing; www.apple.com/imovie/). As with the audio editing tools discussed previously, each of these software programs contains features important to vidcast editors. These include:

- *Storyboard and timeline views* – With each piece of software, the editor can preview the content in either a storyboard or timeline fashion. The storyboard view shows each segment of video as a separate illustration, making it easy to get an idea of the flow of the video and making it easy to move scenes around and add transitions. The timeline view shows the video in a minute and second format, which is useful for editing specific sections of the video.

- *Importing audio and video* – Import music or video that was created separately from the video you are currently editing. You can add background music and intro and outro music, and work with video that was created at different times.
- *Title clips* – This is an easy way to insert the title of the vidcast into your file as well as add credits and other information within the video or at the end of the production.
- *Special effects* – It's easy to add effects after the fact with Adobe Premiere Elements and iMovie. Effects include those required to improve brightness and contrast, as well as transitions and simply fun effects such as "earthquake." These effects can be added to title clips as well as to sections of or an entire movie.

Both iMovie and Adobe Premiere Elements are good low-cost products for beginning vidcasters. They are fairly simple to use, which makes it possible to focus on the quality of the production rather than the way the software works. Your decision on which to purchase is made for you, depending on which operating system you use.

Saving Your Productions

One of the most confusing aspects of podcast production can be the file format in which you need to save what you create. In both audio and video production, it's important to think about the size of the files that you create and make available for subscription and download. It's also essential to consider the format of the file, since you want to make sure that your potential listeners and viewers can access what you create.

Audio File Formats

In order to guarantee that all types of listeners—those who listen on portable media devices as well as those who listen on their

Naming and Tagging Podcast Files

It's a good idea to set up a framework for naming your podcast files so that you always use the same format from episode to episode. One common naming format is to use the title of the podcast and an episode number. For example, a podcast called LibraryCast might use the naming format "library cast_01.mp3" to designate its first episode.

When saving a podcast, it's also important to provide what is called ID3 tag information. Most software programs in which you edit podcasts provide a screen for creating these tags. ID3 tag information is the metadata information for your podcast that includes the title of the podcast episode, author, and a description of the file. When viewing a podcast file in a podcatcher, the ID3 tag title and description is displayed, that is, the listener can see the title and description of the particular podcast episode. This can be very useful for subscribers who want to see an overview of a particular episode or who want to be reminded of the content of a particular episode.

computers—are able to hear the audio that you distribute as a podcast, you will want to save the file in MP3 format. MP3 files can be heard on all types of portable media devices, including iPods and Microsoft Zune, as well as on computers. An MP3 file isn't the highest quality audio file format, but it is compressed, making it smaller than many other types. That means when you distribute the file via your podcast feed, you won't clog up a subscriber's connection while the podcast is downloading.

When creating an audio file in Audacity, files are saved in an AUP format (Audacity Project format). In order to save these files as MP3s, you need to download the LAME encoder found at audacity.sourceforge.net, unzip it, and inform Audacity where the LAME encoder file is stored on your computer. (After you inform Audacity of the file's location once, you don't have to repeat the process in the future.) Instead of saving a file as MP3 in Audacity itself, you can export the file as an MP3.

When using GarageBand, the process may seem a little more complex. GarageBand saves files in GAB format. In order to save them as MP3s, you will need first to share the file with iTunes. (Select "Share" from the GarageBand menu.) From iTunes, select the "advanced" feature, then convert the file to MP3, and you will have your podcast in MP3 format.

Video File Formats

Of course, once you start including moving images along with sound, the size of a file grows. Compressing video for podcasts, so that they are both high quality and available for speedy download, is an art in itself. You can also use iMovie or Adobe Premiere Elements to save your vidcast in a format and file size that won't cause your subscribers bandwidth pain.

Video Compression Tips

Here are a few tips for reducing the size of the video you make available through podcasts:

1. *Reduce the resolution of the video to less than 640x480 pixels* – When you save the video, you will have options for resolution size; you can select something smaller than the default.
2. *Change the frames per second of the video* – If there isn't a lot of movement and action in your production, you can safely reduce the frames per second to below the traditional frame rate of 30 frames per second (30 fps).
3. *Compress the audio* – If your video just includes narration, then you can simply compress the audio as mono instead of stereo.

You can learn more about video compression at the Ars Technica guide to capturing, cleaning, and compressing video (arstechnica.com/guides/tweaks/vidcap.ars).

When editing video in iMovie, the file will be saved in a proprietary iMovie format. Once you save the raw file, you can then export it and select the "Expert Settings." On the next menu, select the "Movie to iPod" item from the dropdown menu. (Don't worry, this doesn't mean the vidcast can only be viewed on an iPod. It does mean it will be saved in QuickTime format for viewing on an iPod or on a computer.) In the next window, select the "Share for Video Podcast" radio button. Then decide where to save the file and what to call it. Once that's done, GarageBand will start converting the video to QuickTime. (This could take a while if the video is a big file.)

In Adobe Premiere Elements, you can export files by selecting Export and then selecting the format in which you want to export the file. QuickTime is a format that provides good compression and is viewable on both computers and portable media devices.

How to Make Your Podcast Accessible

As a podcast producer, you can make your content available to those with hearing and seeing impairments through transcribing your podcast and by captioning the video productions you create.

Transcription

On his podcasting blog, Jeffrey Daniel Frey writes about the technologies available for serving the hearing- and seeing-impaired via podcasts. In an October 2006 post, Frey provides a complete rundown of the services available for podcast transcription. He mentions several factors to consider when working with a transcription service, including:

- *Delivery method* – How do you send the audio to the service, and how do they send the transcription back to you?
- *Timeframe* – How much time does it take to have your audio transcribed?
- *Cost* – What is the per-minute fee for the transcription service? These services are not inexpensive, but they do allow you to serve both hearing and hearing-impaired listeners.

His full blog post on transcription services is available at jdfrey.wordpress.com/2006/10/31/podcasting-transcription-services/.

Captioning

In November 2006, Frey discussed software options for podcast captioning. This can be a time-consuming process, and you will want to make sure to plan for the time it will take to create the captions as you develop a podcast production schedule.

The full blog post on captioning podcasts is available at jdfrey.wordpress.com/2006/11/02/podcast-captioning/.

Publishing and Distributing Your Podcast

Now that you have created your podcast, you need to upload it to a server and distribute it to subscribers. As mentioned previously, PodServe and PodOmatic both provide space for podcast producers to upload and distribute their files. Both sites create a feed for the podcast that can be used by interested listeners or viewers to subscribe.

PodServe and PodOmatic are free Web-hosting options for getting your podcast on someone else's server, but your library might already have a blog you can use to publish your podcast. Many blog-hosting services also provide a podcasting component. For example, blogging products from Six Apart (www.sixapart.com) provide podcasting integration, and MySpace blogs include the ability to upload a podcast to the blog.

If you don't use one of these Web-based tools, you'll need to have space on a server where you can upload your podcast files. You'll want to make sure there is enough space for your productions on the server and that the bandwidth limitations of the server don't impede your subscribers' ability to download your latest episodes. When multiple subscribers download a podcast all at once, they can use up a lot of bandwidth. The server you use will have to be able to handle that.

iTunes U

Apple gives colleges and universities the opportunity to upload audio and video content to Apple's servers and to make that content available to students for download and transfer to portable media devices. A number of institutions, including Stanford University and the University of California at Berkeley, use this technology to get content to their students. More information is available on the Apple site at www.apple.com/education/products/ipod/itunes_u.html.

The next thing you'll have to do is to create an RSS feed for potential listeners and viewers to subscribe to in order to find out when you have a new episode available. FeedBurner (www.feedburner.com/fb/a/home) is a free service that provides distribution of podcasts that already have a feed. FeedBurner, though, doesn't leave you hanging if you don't already have an RSS feed. The site links to several tutorials on how to create feeds using a variety of different Web hosts; it also has information on where you can have your podcasts hosted.

Creating an RSS Feed: The Basics

At the core of each RSS feed is an XML file that distributes information to a feed reader whenever new content is available. In most cases, you want to automate that updating process so that someone doesn't have to change the XML file manually whenever new podcast content is available. A service like FeedBurner automates the process for you. However, the first step is to create the XML file.

As previously mentioned, if you use a blog to host your podcast show notes, it is very likely there is an XML feed already embedded in the software you are using. You can easily use FeedBurner to set up a feed for a podcast that uses a blog for hosting and show notes.

1. Set up a FeedBurner account (it's free).
2. Go to your show notes blog, and copy the URL. Then, go to the FeedBurner site (www.feedburner.com/fb/a/podcasts#burnNow), and paste the URL into the space provided. Select the checkbox for "I am a podcaster," and click on "Next."
3. If the next screen provides a selection of feed sources, select RSS 2.0. (This is the second version of the RSS language, which is readable by a variety of feed readers.)
4. Enter a title for the feed and select the address for the feed. (This is the URL that subscribers will use to subscribe to your feed.)
5. Once the feed is created, you'll have the option to add more specific information about your podcast. The next screen gives you the chance to upload the image that you want to have displayed when people listen to your cast, decide if you want to be listed in iTunes and Yahoo!, write a description for the production, and add copyright information. You can choose how much or how little of this information you add to your feed.
6. The final setup screen gives you the chance to decide what statistics you want to keep for your podcast. This information can be very helpful when seeking support from colleagues, administrators, and community members.
7. Once your feed is set up at FeedBurner, the site will regularly go out and check your content to discover if anything new has been uploaded.

If you need to create an XML file by hand before using FeedBurner for distribution, you can learn how to do that step-by-step by using "How to Create RSS/XML Feeds for Podcasts" (www.podcast411.com/howto_1.html).

Now What?

Now that you have read about information on what it takes to create your podcast, you still might wonder how you are going to get people to listen to or view your podcast. In the next chapter, I provide tips for getting people to do just that.

Endnotes

1. Leo Laporte, "Podcasting Equipment," TWiT.TV, www.twit.tv/podcast equipment (accessed December 20, 2006).
2. Barett Golding, "Recording Highs and Lows," Atlanta Public Media, www.transom.org/tools/recording_interviewing/200101.recording.bgolding.html (accessed November 27, 2006).
3. Emily Price, "Basic Camcorder Shooting Tips," About Inc., camcorders.about.com/od/videorecordingtips/a/ShootingTips.htm (accessed November 27, 2006).

CHAPTER 6

Get the Word Out

No one wants to throw a party that no one attends—and no one wants to produce a podcast that no one listens to. Once podcast production starts, it's a good idea to begin getting the word out so that people will look forward to your production, want to subscribe, and spread news of your program by word-of-mouth.

This chapter looks at how you can use technology, other podcasters' productions, and online social networks to get the word out about your podcasts to potential listeners and viewers.

Use Show Notes Well

Since potential as well as current listeners can learn about a podcast from the show notes Web site, the site becomes an important marketing tool for podcasters. It's a way to sell the content of a podcast and provide an idea of the tone and format of the show. The best show notes sites provide a feel for each podcast episode instead of only listing the names of the shows. For example, a show notes site might include a sentence about each link that reflects how content was discussed in the podcast episode.

Examples of show notes that act as marketing tools as well as lists of podcast content include:

- Buzz Out Loud, alpha.cnet.com – Buzz Out Loud is a daily podcast that covers technology news. The feedback from listeners that appears at the end of every show notes page acts as a great marketing tool. By reading the comments, visitors get an idea of what the content of the show is like, what listeners think of that content, and how the hosts respond to questions.
- Daily SearchCast, dailysearchcast.com – The show notes for Daily SearchCast are incredibly rich. Each episode's

notes include an overview of the content, followed by the title of each story, a link to the Web site associated with the story, and a full rundown of the content of the story. This gives potential listeners a full understanding of the types of topics covered and the perspective of the podcast hosts. From the front page of the Daily SearchCast show notes site, select the "More" link to read the full content of the notes for a particular podcast.

Don't forget that you want to make it as easy as possible for visitors to your show notes Web site to be able to subscribe to your podcast via the site. One way to do this is by displaying subscription links for popular podcatchers prominently on your site. (See Chapter 1 for examples of podcast feed logos.) You should also include a frequently asked questions file or similar resource for visitors who might not know what they have to do in order to subscribe to a podcast. For example, the Cheshire Public Library podcast page (www.cheshirelib.org/teens/cplpodcast.htm) includes links at the bottom to documents explaining podcasting and how subscribing to podcasts works.

Get Into Podcast Directories

A podcast directory is a searchable and browsable Web site that lists podcasts. (These include iTunes, Odeo, and Yahoo!'s Podcast Search, which are described in Chapter 1.) One feature common to these directories is that the front page of the search tool highlights favorite podcasts of both listeners and the directory's staff. It can be a dream come true to be highlighted on a podcast directory's front page. It's not necessary, though, to be on the front page in order to bring in listeners and viewers. Here are a few simple ways to make sure your podcast is uncovered by podcast directory users:

- Make sure to use your ID3 tags wisely. (You can read about ID3 tags in Chapter 5.) When you describe the podcast as a whole, use the terms and phrases you think potential listeners might use when looking for a podcast like yours. The same goes when describing each episode; use specific keywords to describe each important topic. Make sure to add keyword ID3 tags that describe both the content of your podcast as a whole and of each episode to make it easy to find your podcast in a directory.

- Visit the podcast directory sites and submit your podcast feed to each. The Yahoo! Podcast directory includes a text box in the "Publish a Podcast" section for submitting the address of your podcast's RSS feed. Odeo provides an "Add a Feed" link on various pages of the site. The iTunes Store has a form visitors can fill out to add a podcast to the directory; within the podcasts section of the store, select the link titled "Submit a Podcast."
- Make sure to place your podcast in the right genre categories in the podcast directories. List your podcast in the categories that are obvious fits, as well as those that may not seem so obvious but which potential subscribers might think of when looking for a podcast like the one you produce.
- When creating your XML for the podcast RSS feed make sure to include the specific XML tags used to categorize and describe a podcast in XML-capable directories such as iTunes. (See Appendix C for an example of an XML file with iTunes-specific XML tags.)

Don't Forget to Vote

Tap into your audience for marketing opportunities as well:

- Some podcast directories, such as Podcast Alley (www.podcastalley.com), give listeners a chance to vote for their favorite podcasts. Take advantage of these and ask your listeners to vote for your podcast.
- iTunes includes a mechanism for podcast listeners and viewers to write podcast reviews. Link to your entry in the iTunes store and ask your subscribers to write reviews.

Get Other Podcasters to Sell Your Podcast

When I first started listening to podcasts, one way I learned about what was available was by hearing promos for other podcasts played on the Daily Source Code. Podcasters send the host, Adam Curry, promos of their shows; if they appeal to him, he plays them. This can be a great way to learn about new podcasts.

Fellow podcasters can act as marketers for your podcast, and you can act as marketer for their podcasts. I'm always learning about podcasts that other podcasters listen to when they mention their listening habits on their shows. I also learn about podcasts from the comments left on podcast show notes sites or discussed in an episode. Don't be afraid to communicate with your fellow podcasters; let them know what you are podcasting, and add links in your podcast information to the comments you leave on others' show notes sites.

One of the best ways to market your podcast is by creating buzz. You'll get that buzz going if you let other podcasters know what you are doing and are willing to reciprocate.

Use Social Networking

You may feel that sites like MySpace (www.myspace.com) are a thing of the past or only for those of a certain generation. Still, you do want to harness the power of social networking technologies to get the word out about your podcast. Consider these ideas:

- Use MySpace bulletins to get the word out to "friends" about your podcast when you first launch, and continue to use MySpace to send out bulletins about upcoming or new episodes.
- Invite listeners to use the social bookmarking Web site del.icio.us (del.icio.us) to let you know about content they'd like you to talk about. For example, in the first episode of net@nite (www.twit.tv/itn), the hosts suggested that listeners add links to del.icio.us with the tag "natn" to suggest what the hosts should talk about on the podcast. Whenever the hosts search for "natn" on del.icio.us, they learn what topics their listeners are interested in. Similarly, listeners learn about topics others who listen to net@nite are interested in, because they too can search del.icio.us to see what's been added. This is a good way to market the podcast, and is also a way to build community around a specific podcast.
- Use Technorati (www.technorati.com) to show the blogs that are linking to your podcast. In order to do this, set up a Technorati account and then add the URL of your podcast

Web site to the Technorati directory. Then whenever anyone whose blog is included in Technorati blogs about your podcast, that link will show up in your Technorati account. On your show notes site, you can link to your Technorati account in order to show potential listeners and viewers what others are saying about your podcast.

What Are MySpace Bulletins?

MySpace bulletins are a great tool for getting the word out about something you have going on at the library or in a school. Anyone who has a MySpace account can post a bulletin, which is sent out to everyone on the poster's "friends" list. For example, if the Hennepin County Library posts a bulletin about a new podcast they have available, I will see the bulletin appear on my main MySpace administrative page—since I am a friend of the Hennepin County Library.

Ask for and Publish Feedback

People will be more invested in your podcast, and more interested in listening or viewing, if they know their thoughts and feedback are welcome. Current listeners will want to listen to a show where they think a comment they made might be discussed—or even played, if audio feedback is available. They will also tell their friends to listen or watch.

As mentioned previously, comments on blog show notes pages are a good way to give listeners and viewers a chance to give their feedback on the podcast. Some podcasters set up a phone number that records calls; that feedback can then be edited into a future podcast episode. Podcast Ready's FeedCaster software (www.podcastready.com/tools.php) provides the ability for podcasters to integrate audio feedback into a show notes site.

Use Traditional Marketing Techniques

Some traditional marketing techniques will work perfectly well for promoting your podcast; they just might need a little bit of tweaking. For example:

- *Create business cards that are just for your podcast* – Hand these out all over the place and make sure they include the show notes URL, the RSS feed URL, the title of the podcast, and a short overview of content.
- *Use traditional media outlets* – Contact local or school newspapers, local access TV stations, and news stations to let them know about your podcast, and ask them to interview you about what you are doing. Highlight the fact you are using cutting-edge technology to meet the needs of those that you serve.
- *Create a logo for your podcast that will attract people visually to what you have to offer* – Make sure to include the logo on all of your marketing materials, on the show notes Web pages, in articles that are published about your podcast, and in your podcast file that is downloaded to listeners' podcatchers.

Market to Your Audience

Don't try to sell your podcast to the entire world. Remember that in your planning stages you determined your podcast's target audience. When deciding what marketing techniques to use, focus on those that would work best for the audience you are trying to serve. For example, if your listeners or viewers aren't likely to be users of social networking sites, then don't use those marketing techniques (at least in the beginning). If your listeners or viewers are parents of preschoolers, make sure to get the word out to preschools and school-related organizations in the community. Distribute materials in the locations where those parents are likely to be, make sure the children's librarian and preschool teachers talk about the podcast to parents, attend parent nights at the local school, and put information in newsletters targeted to preschool parents.

It's Worth It

While marketing your podcast might take a lot of time and might require some out-of-the-box thinking, in the long run it will be well worth it. With effective marketing your podcast can become a primary way that the people you serve learn about what you do, what your institution has to offer, and how you can make a difference in the lives of the people in your community. You want the listeners and/or viewers of your podcast to get a sense of what the library or school in which you work is all about. You want listeners and viewers to know that the people who work in your institution are real people. So, get out there and sell what you have to offer by using these techniques.

Podcast Planning Worksheet

1. Why do you want to do a podcast? What do you hope to achieve from your podcasts?
2. Who is your target audience?
3. Where will your podcast live? (What is the podcast URL?)
4. What is the podcast feed URL?
5. How often will you produce and distribute your podcast?
   - ☐ Weekly
   - ☐ Monthly
   - ☐ Every other month
   - ☐ Irregularly
6. How long will the podcast be?
   - ☐ Less than 10 minutes
   - ☐ 10 to 20 minutes
   - ☐ 20 to 40 minutes
   - ☐ Over 40 minutes
7. What topics will your podcast cover? (Check all that apply)
   - ☐ Library collections (for example, reviews of materials, information on new materials)

- ☐ Library news (for example, upcoming programs and events)
- ☐ Library instruction (how to use library tools and resources)
- ☐ Recordings of library programs
- ☐ Interviews with community members
- ☐ Student-created content
- ☐ Other ________________________________

8. Will music be included in the podcast?

   - ☐ Yes
   - ☐ No

   If yes, where will you get the music that you use?

   - ☐ IODA Promonet, promonet.iodalliance.com/login.php
   - ☐ Magnatune, magnatune.com/info/podcast
   - ☐ Podsafe Audio, www.podsafeaudio.com
   - ☐ The Podsafe Music Network, music.podshow.com
   - ☐ Other ________________________________

9. How do you want podcast listeners to describe your podcast? (Check all that apply)

   - ☐ Formal
   - ☐ Informal
   - ☐ Educational
   - ☐ Entertaining
   - ☐ Funny
   - ☐ Informative
   - ☐ Useful
   - ☐ Other ________________________________

10. Where will you submit your podcast for listing? (Check all that apply)

    - ☐ iTunes
    - ☐ Yahoo!
    - ☐ Odeo
    - ☐ Podcast Alley
    - ☐ Other ______________________________

11. What methods will you use to get the word out about your podcast? (Check all that apply)

    - ☐ Show notes site
    - ☐ Institutional Web site
    - ☐ Other podcasts
    - ☐ Social networking sites
    - ☐ Feedback mechanisms
    - ☐ Business cards
    - ☐ Articles in local media
    - ☐ Other ______________________________

APPENDIX B

Podcasting Tools

Audio Recording and Editing

This list includes some of the software you might want to try out when recording and editing podcasts:

Audacity, audacity.sourceforge.net
Audio Hijack, www.rogueamoeba.com/audiohijack/
GarageBand, www.apple.com/ilife/garageband/
Sound Recorder, www.soundrecorder.net

Recording VoIP

If you are using Skype or another software tool to bring people in disparate locations together for a podcast recording, consider using Audacity or one of the following software options:

Call Recorder, www.ecamm.com/mac/callrecorder
Hot Recorder, www.hotrecorder.com

Video Editing

When you are ready to edit your video, one of these software programs will give you the tools you need:

Adobe Premiere Elements, www.adobe.com/products/premiereel/index.html
iMovie, www.apple.com/ilife/imovie
Ulead Video Studio, www.ulead.com/vs/

Screencasting

Two software programs are most often used for screencasting (both are only available for Windows):

Camtasia, www.techsmith.com/camtasia.asp
Captivate, www.adobe.com/products/captivate

RSS and XML

Learn more about RSS and how to create an XML RSS feed with these resources:

Making a Podcast with Blogger and FeedBurner, www.podcastingnews.com/articles/Make_Podcast_Blogger.html
Making an RSS Feed, searchenginewatch.com/showPage.html?page=2175271
RSS Tutorial, www.w3schools.com/rss/default.asp
Wikipedia: RSS, en.wikipedia.org/wiki/RSS_%28file_format%29

Music Licensing

Find music for your podcast that is Creative Commons licensed and read about music licensing for podcasts at the resources listed here:

Creative Commons: Audio, creativecommons.org/audio
IODA Promonet, promonet.iodalliance.com/login.php
Magnatune, magnatune.com/info/podcast
Podcasting Legal Guide, creativecommons.org/podcasting
Podsafe Audio, www.podsafeaudio.com
Podsafe Music Network, music.podshow.com

Podcast and Show Notes Hosts

Looking for a place to host your podcast? Looking for a place to host your show notes? Try one of these:

Blogger, www.blogger.com
iTunes U, www.apple.com/education/products/ipod/itunes_u.html
Libsyn, www.libsyn.com
Movable Type, www.movabletype.com
OurMedia, www.ourmedia.org

Podbus, podbus.com
PodOmatic, www.podomatic.com
PodServe, www.pod-serve.com

Podcast Directories

Need to find podcasts? Check out these resources:
iTunes, www.itunes.com
Odeo, www.odeo.com
Podcast Alley, www.podcastalley.com
Yahoo! Podcasts, podcasts.yahoo.com

Podcatchers

Subscribe to and download podcasts with one of these software programs:
Doppler, www.dopplerradio.net
FireAnt, getfireant.com
iTunes, www.itunes.com
jPodder, www.jpodder.com
Juice, juicereceiver.sourceforge.net

Sample Podcast Feed

XML stands for Xtensible Markup Language and is a programming language for creating interactive Web content. It looks very much like HTML. XML code includes opening and closing tags (inside the < and >); in an RSS feed, these define information about the podcast. This information includes the name of the podcast, the name of a podcast episode, a description of the podcast, the image that should be used with the podcast, and information for iTunes about how to display the podcast content in the podcatcher. An example of an XML file for a podcast is below; notes highlight different sections of the code and what they mean.

```
<?xml version="1.0" encoding="iso-8859-1"?>
<rss xmlns:itunes="http://www.itunes.com/DTDs/Podcast-1.0.dtd" version="2.0"
xmlns:media="http://search.yahoo.com/mrss"
xmlns:feedburner="http://rssnamespace.org/feedburner/ext/1.0">
  <channel>
    <title>YALSA Podcasts</title>
    <link>0</link>
    <itunes:author>YALSA</itunes:author>
    <itunes:subtitle>A series of podcasts produced by the Young Adult Library
Association. On topics related to teens, technology, and libraries. For nearly 50 years,
YALSA has been the world leader in selecting books, videos, and audio books for teens.
For more information about YALSA or for lists of recommended reading, viewing and
listening, go to www.ala.org/yalsa/booklists, or contact the YALSA office by phone, 800-
545-2433, ext. 4390; or e-mail: yalsa@ala.org. </itunes:subtitle>
    <itunes:summary>A series of podcasts produced by the Young Adult Library
Association. On topics related to teens, technology, and libraries. For nearly 50 years,
YALSA has been the world leader in selecting books, videos, and audio books for teens.
For more information about YALSA or for lists of recommended reading, viewing and
listening, go to www.ala.org/yalsa/booklists, or contact the YALSA office by phone, 800-
545-2433, ext. 4390; or e-mail: yalsa@ala.org. </itunes:summary>

    <itunes:description>A series of podcasts produced by the Young Adult Library
Association. On topics related to teens, technology, and libraries. For nearly 50 years,
YALSA has been the world leader in selecting books, videos, and audio books for teens.
For more information about YALSA or for lists of recommended reading, viewing and
listening, go to www.ala.org/yalsa/booklists, or contact the YALSA office by phone, 800-
545-2433, ext. 4390; or e-mail: yalsa@ala.org. </itunes:description>
    <language>en-us</language>
    <copyright>Copyright 2005 lbraun2000</copyright>
```

Name of the podcast.

Podcast author for iTunes

Description, summary, and subtitle for iTunes

```
<itunes:image href="http://pod-serve.com/podcast/coverart/1604/YALSAnew2.gif"/>
<image>
  <url>http://pod-serve.com/podcast/coverart/1604/YALSAnew2.gif</url>
  <title>YALSA Podcasts</title>
```

Image displayed in directories and iTunes

```
  <link>0</link>
  <width>170</width>
  <height>170</height>
</image>
<itunes:owner>
  <itunes:name>yalsa</itunes:name>
  <itunes:email>yalsa@ala.org</itunes:email>

</itunes:owner>
<itunes:category>Learning &amp; Instruction</itunes:category>
```

Category podcast is listed under in iTunes

```
<itunes:explicit xmlns:itunes="http://www.itunes.com/dtds/podcast-
1.0.dtd">No</itunes:explicit>
<itunes:image xmlns:itunes="http://www.itunes.com/dtds/podcast-1.0.dtd">http://pod-
serve.com/podcast/coverart/1604/YALSAnew2.gif</itunes:image>
<item>
```

Info. on the most recent podcast available for download -- between <item> and </item

```
  <title>YALSA Podcast #4 Gaming Interest Group</title>

  <itunes:author>yalsa</itunes:author>
  <itunes:subtitle>An overview of the YALSA Gaming Interest Group meeting at
Annual Conference 2006.</itunes:subtitle>
  <itunes:summary>An overview of the YALSA Gaming Interest Group meeting at
Annual Conference 2006.</itunes:summary>
  <link>http://pod-
serve.com/audiofile/filename/3930/gallaway_gaming_podcast_1.mp3</link>
  <description>An overview of the YALSA Gaming Interest Group meeting at Annual
Conference 2006.</description>
  <pubDate>2006-11-27</pubDate>

  <itunes:author>lbraun2000</itunes:author>
  <enclosure url="http://pod-
serve.com/audiofile/filename/3930/gallaway_gaming_podcast_1.mp3"
type="audio/mpeg" lenght="3734146"/>
  <guid>http://pod-
serve.com/audiofile/filename/3930/gallaway_gaming_podcast_1.mp3</guid>
  <itunes:category>Learning &amp; Instruction</itunes:category>
  <itunes:keywords></itunes:keywords>
  <media:content url="http://pod-
serve.com/audiofile/filename/3930/gallaway_gaming_podcast_1.mp3"
type="audio/mpeg">

    <media:adult scheme="urn:simple">nonadult</media:adult>
  </media:content>
  <itunes:explicit xmlns:itunes="http://www.itunes.com/dtds/podcast-
1.0.dtd">No</itunes:explicit>
  <itunes:subtitle xmlns:itunes="http://www.itunes.com/dtds/podcast-1.0.dtd">An
overview of the YALSA Gaming Interest Group meeting at Annual Conference
2006.</itunes:subtitle>
  <itunes:summary xmlns:itunes="http://www.itunes.com/dtds/podcast-1.0.dtd">An
overview of the YALSA Gaming Interest Group meeting at Annual Conference
2006.</itunes:summary>
</item>
```

Glossary

Digital Voice Recorder. A tape recorder—minus the tape. The recording is made in a digital format that can then be uploaded to a computer for editing, listening, or posting on the Web.

Enclosure. A file included as a part of an RSS feed delivery. (See definition of **RSS**.) Enclosures can be audio, video, or print files (such as PDFs).

Feed reader. A piece of software or Web-based tool that collects the RSS feeds someone subscribes to. The feed reader goes out and collects new information on a regular basis and delivers it to the subscriber. NetNewsWire and NewsGator are examples of RSS feed readers.

ID3 tags. Pieces of information included with a podcast file that inform listeners of podcast content. This can include the author of the podcast, the subject of a podcast, and the description of a podcast episode.

MP3 (MPEG-1 Audio Layer 3). An audio file format that is readable by computers and most portable audio devices.

OPML (Outline Processor Markup Language). A file format that allows people to exchange podcast and RSS subscriptions. An OPML file created by one listener or reader can be imported by another listener or reader into their podcatcher or feed reader.

Podcast. An audio or video file that is hosted on the Web and available for subscription to potential listeners or viewers.

Podcatcher. A piece of software or Web-based tool that makes it possible to subscribe to podcasts. iTunes, Juice, and jPodder are examples of podcatchers.

Portable media device. Small units onto which listeners and viewers can download audio and/or video content. The iPod, the Zune, and the iRiver are examples of portable media devices.

RSS (Really Simple Syndication or Rich Site Summary). The technology used that makes it possible for people to subscribe to podcasts and text-based RSS feeds.

Screencast. This term is used to designate movement on a computer screen that is captured and made available for playback on a local computer, on the Web, or via a podcast.

Show notes. A Web-based companion to a podcast is usually comprised of notes. These notes provide information on what was included in a podcast and include links to resources discussed in a podcast.

Vidcast. One of the terms used to describe a podcast that is in video form.

Vodcast (Video on Demand cast). One of the terms used to describe a podcast that is in video form.

VoIP (Voice Over Internet Protocol). This technology allows users to make an audio call from one computer to another. Podcasters use VoIP to record people in different locations. Skype is an example of VoIP software.

WAV (Waveform Audio Format). An audio file format that is standard for saving files and playing them back on a computer.

WMA (Windows Media Audio). WMA is an audio file format commonly used when recording and playing back using Microsoft devices. There are products that allow those who use Apple products to listen to WMA audio or convert WMA audio to an Apple compatible format.

XML (Extensible Markup Language). A programming language used in creating RSS feeds for text, audio, and video.

Resources

Podcasts

Alpha Blog: Buzz (C|NET Networks, Inc.), alpha.cnet.com

Ask a Ninja (Kent Nichols and Douglas Sarine), www.askaninja.com

Cheshire Public Library Podcasts (Cheshire Public Library), www.cheshirelib.org/teens/cplpodcast.htm

Coverville (Brian Ibbott), coverville.com

Cranky Geeks (John C. Dvorak), Ziff Davis Internet, www.cranky geeks.com

Daily Giz Wiz (Leo Laporte, TWiT.TV), gizwiz.biz

Daily SearchCast (Danny Sullivan and Webmaster Radio, Inc.), www.dailysearchcast.com

Daily Source Code (Adam Curry), PodShow, Inc., www.dailysource code.com

Diggnation (Revision3 Corporation), revision3.com/diggnation

Dowling College Podcasts (Dowling College), www.dowling.edu/library/newsblog/podcasts.asp

Hennepin County Podcasts (Hennepin County Library), www.hclib.org/teens/Podcasts.cfm

Kankakee Public Library Podcasts (Kankakee Public Library), www.lions-online.org/podcasts.html

MommyCast (KDCP Productions, LLC), www.mommycast.com

net@nite (TWiT.TV), www.twit.tv/itn

New York Times: David Pogue (New York Times), www.nytimes.com/ref/multimedia/podcasts.html#pogue

Official *Lost* Podcast (ABC), abc.go.com/primetime/lost/podcast

On the Media (WNYC Radio), www.onthemedia.org

Podcast for Teachers (Kathy King and Mark Gura, Fordham University RETC Center For Professional Development), www.podcastforteachers.com

Rocketboom (Andrew Baron), www.rocketboom.com

School in the Coulee Student Podcast (Longfellow Middle School, School District of LaCrosse, Wisconsin), www.sdlax.net/longfellow/sc/ck/index.htm

Search Engine Watch (Danny Sullivan, Incisive Interactive Marketing), www.searchenginewatch.com

Second Life (Linden Labs), www.secondlife.com

This Week in Tech (Leo Laporte TWiT.TV), www.twit.tv/twit

TV Guide Talk (TV Guide Online Inc.), www.tvguide.com/News-Views/TVGuide-Talk/Podcasts/default.aspx

WillowWeb Radio (Willowdale Elementary School, Millard School District), www.mpsomaha.org/willow/radio

YALSA Podcast #3 (Cheshire Public Library), pod-serve.com/audiofile/filename/3806/cpl_podcast.mp3

YALSA Podcast #5 (Stephanies ISER), pod-serve.com/audiofile/filename/4111/creative_commons_music.mp3

Software and Tools

Audacity (Audacity Development Team), audacity.sourceforge.net

Audio Highjack Pro (Rogue Amoeba Software, LLC), www.rogueamoeba.com/audiohijack/

FeedBurner (FeedBurner, Inc.), www.feedburner.com/fb/a/help/podcast_quickstart

GarageBand (Apple Computer, Inc.), www.apple.com/ilife/garageband

Google Calendar, calendar.google.com

IODA Promonet (Independent Online Distribution Alliance), promonet.iodalliance.com/login.php

iTunes U (Apple Computer, Inc.), www.apple.com/education/products/ipod/itunes_u.html

Magnatune, magnatune.com/info/podcast

Odeo (Obvious Corp.), www.odeo.com

Podcast Alley, (Chris McIntyre), www.podcastalley.com

Podcast Ready, www.podcastready.com/tools.php

Podcasting Equipment (Leo Laporte, TWiT.TV), www.twit.tv/podcast equipment

Podlinez (Podlinez Incorporated), www.podlinez.com

Podsafe Audio, www.podsafeaudio.com

Podsafe Music Network (PodShow, Inc.), music.podshow.com

Pod-Serve (Big in Japan), www.pod-serve.com

Podzinger (BBN Technologies, Corp.), www.podzinger.com

Skype (Skype Limited), www.skype.com

Technorati (Technorati, Inc.), www.technorati.com

TWiT on del.icio.us, del.icio.us/twit

Yahoo! Podcasts, podcasts.yahoo.com

Articles and Blogs

Golding, Barrett. "Recording Highs and Lows." Transom.org. Atlanta Public Media. www.transom.org/tools/recording_interviewing/200101.recording.bgolding.html

Goodstein, Anastasia. Ypulse. www.ypulse.com

"History of Podcasting." Wikipedia. en.wikipedia.org/wiki/History_of_Podcasting

Pew Internet and American Life Project. "Podcast Downloading." www.pewinternet.org/PPF/r/193/report_display.asp

Price, Emily. “Basic Camcorder Shooting Tips.” About, Inc., camcorders.about.com/od/videorecordingtips/a/ShootingTips.htm

Books

Farkas, Bart G. *Secrets of Podcasting: Audio Blogging for the Masses.* Berkeley, CA: Peachpit Press, 2006.

Geoghegan, Michael W. and Dan Klass. *Podcast Solutions: The Complete Guide to Podcasting.* Berkeley, CA: Friends of Ed, 2005.

Herrington, Jack D. *Podcasting Hacks: Tips & Tools for Blogging Out Loud.* Sebastopol. CA: O’Reilly Media Inc., 2005.

About the Author

Linda W. Braun is an educational technology consultant with LEO: Librarians & Educators Online. Through her job, she works with schools, libraries, and other types of educational institutions to help them figure out the best way to integrate technology into their programs and services. She is also an adjunct faculty member at Simmons College Graduate School of Library and Information Science where she teaches young adult and technology classes.

Linda provides project management and consulting services to public libraries and schools on a variety of topics, and she has experience in curriculum and Web site development. Linda has a Master of Science degree in Library and Information Science from Simmons College and a Master of Education with a specialization in Computers in Education from Lesley University.

Linda's publications include *Introducing the Internet to Young Learners: Ready-To-Go Activities And Lesson Plans, The Browsable Classroom: An Introduction to E-Learning For Librarians,* and *Hooking Teens with the Net* (each published by Neal-Schuman Publishers, Inc.). Her books published by the American Library Association are *Teens.Library: Developing Internet Services for Young Adults* and *Technically Involved: Technology-Based Youth Participation Activities for Your Library.* In December 2006, her book *Teens, Technology & Literacy* was published by Libraries Unlimited. Linda has also authored articles for journals including *netConnect, Library Journal,* and *School Library Journal,* and is a columnist for *VOYA.*

Index

K

L

M

N

O

P

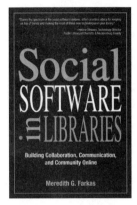

Blogging & RSS

A Librarian's Guide

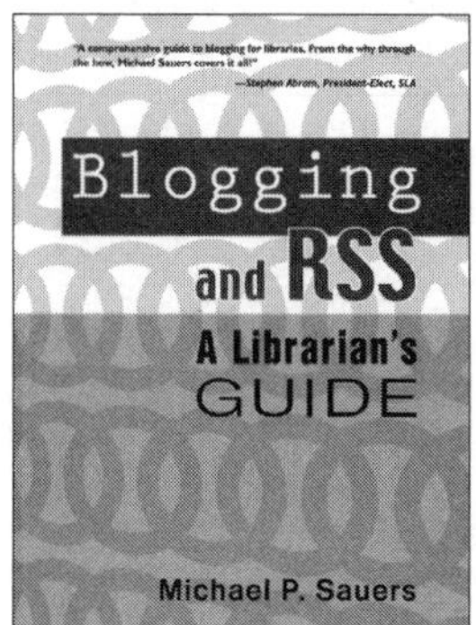

By Michael P. Sauers

Author, Internet trainer, and blogger Michael P. Sauers shows how blogging and RSS can be easily and effectively used in the context of a library community. Sauers showcases interesting and useful blogs, shares insights from librarian bloggers, and offers step-by-step instructions for creating, publishing, and syndicating a blog using free Web-based services, software, RSS feeds, and aggregators.

288 pp/softbound/ISBN 978-1-57387-268-3 $29.50

Library 2.0

A Guide to Participatory Library Service

By Michael E. Casey and Laura C. Savastinuk

Two of the first and most original thinkers on Library 2.0 introduce the essential concepts and offer ways to improve service to better meet the changing needs of 21st-century library users. Describing a service model of constant and purposeful change, evaluation and updating of library services, and user participation, the book both outlines the theoretical underpinnings of Library 2.0 and provides practical advice on how to get there.

200 pp/softbound/ISBN 978-1-57387-297-3 $29.50